I0462162

PRESTON

VOLUME TWO

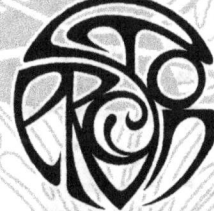

Copyright © 2019 by Dennis Preston
All rights reserved

ISBN 978-0-359-23564-3

The collection of illustrations in this book comes from:
CRITTERS,CREATURES & CUTIES
PRESTON POTPOURRI Volume One
PRESTON POTPOURRI Volume Two
PRESTON POTPOURRI Volume Three
AND... a few Bonus Drawings
for this book only!

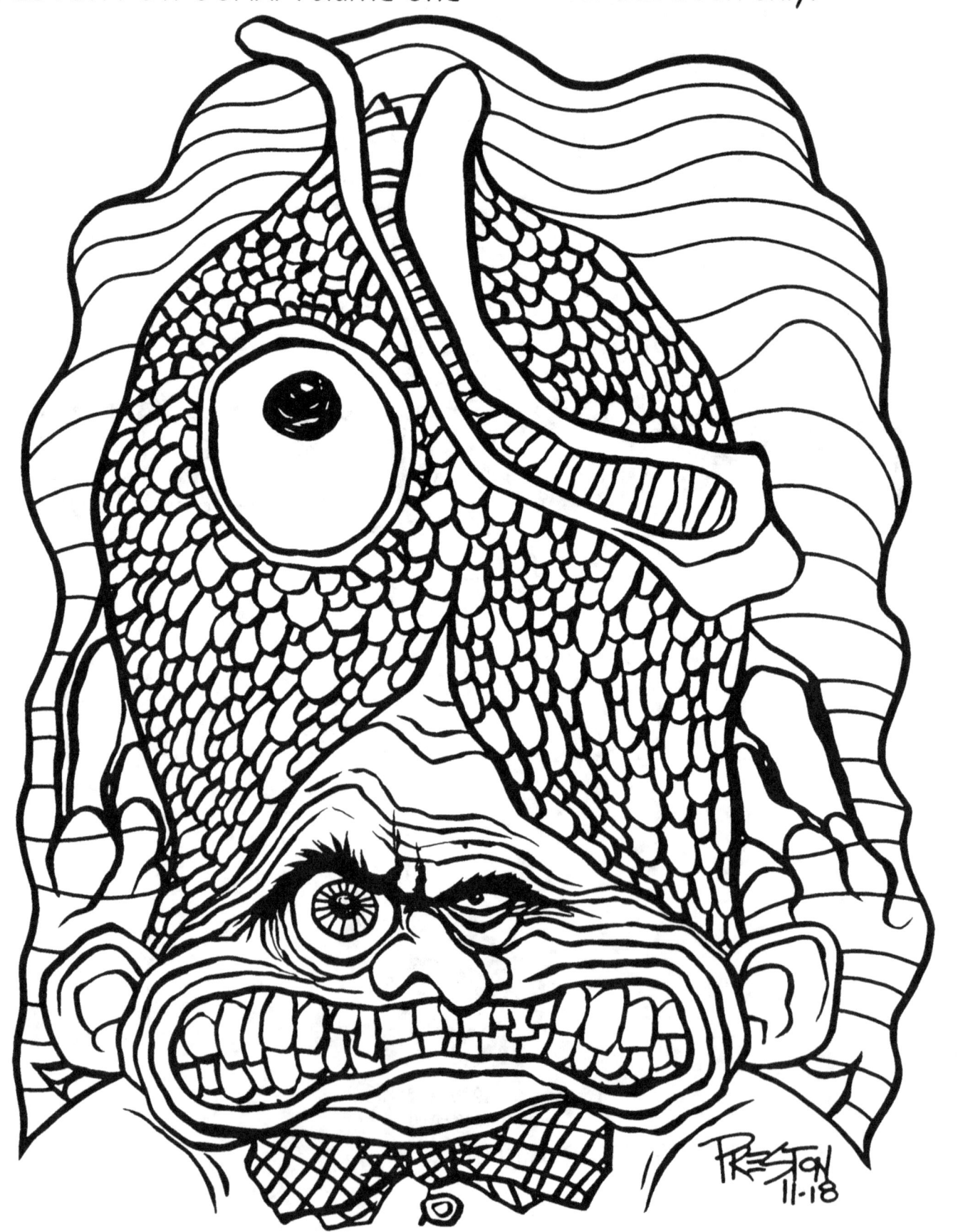

PRESTON
11-18

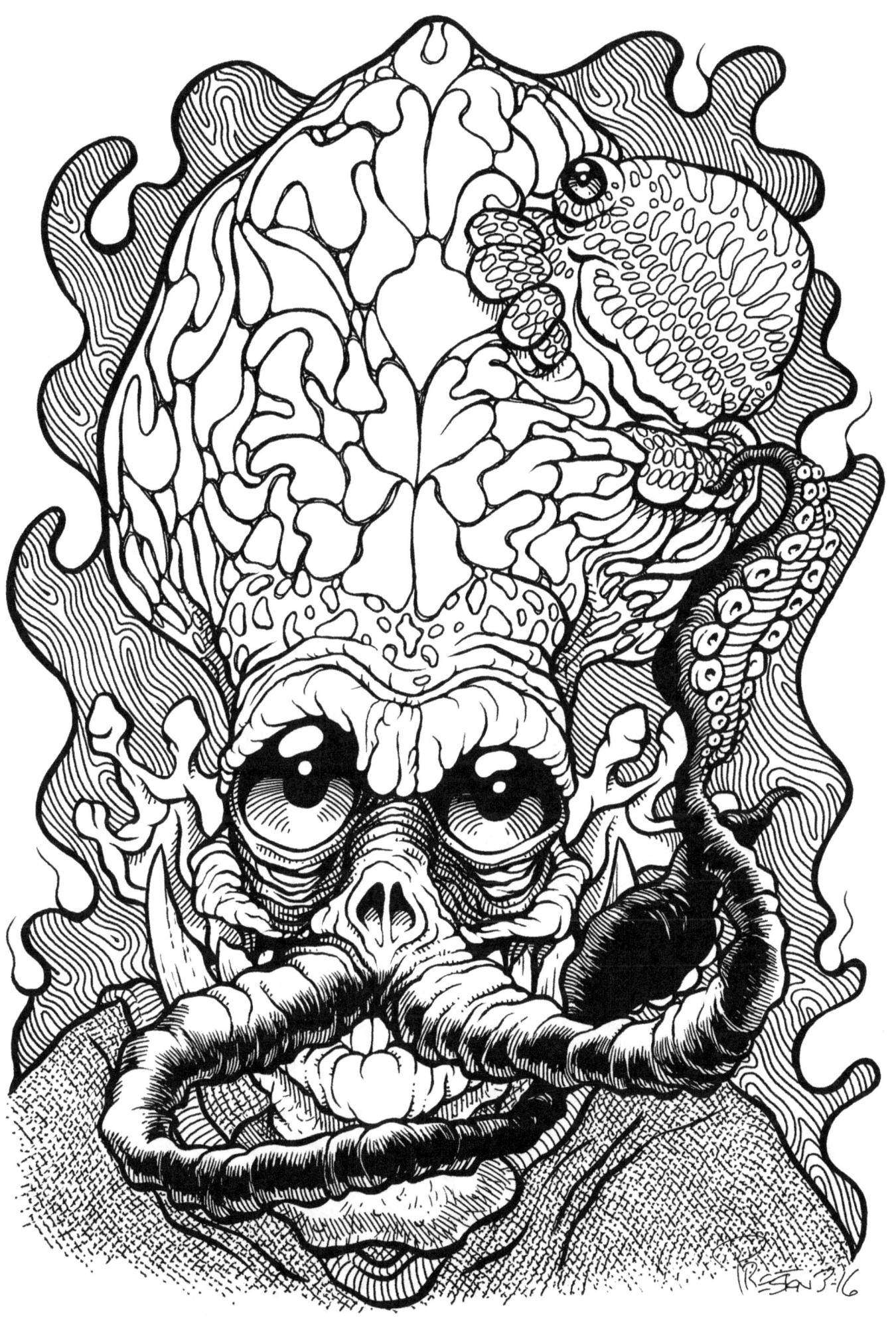

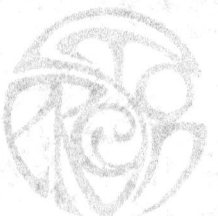

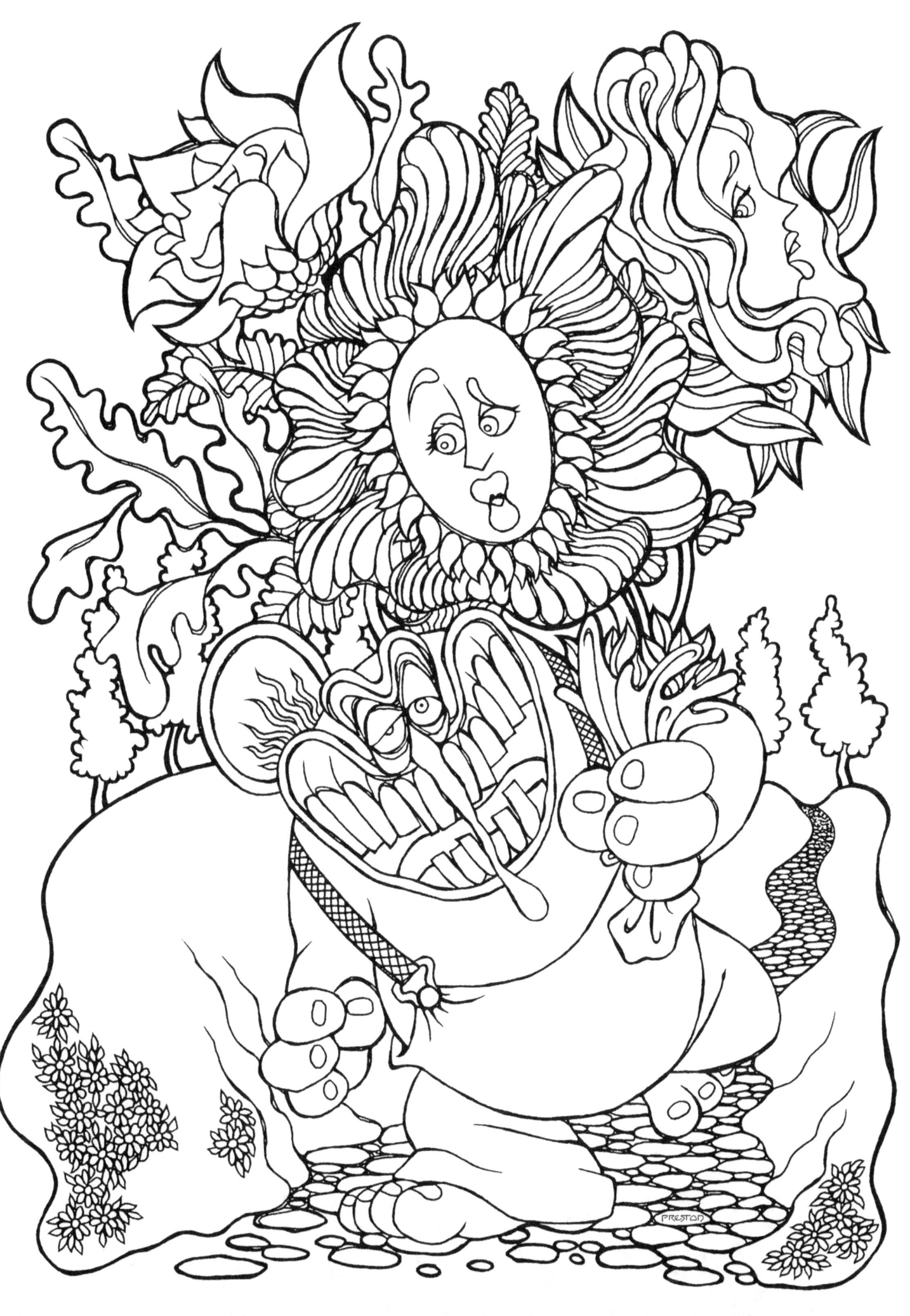

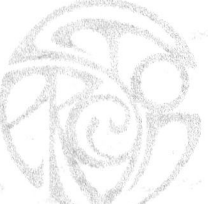

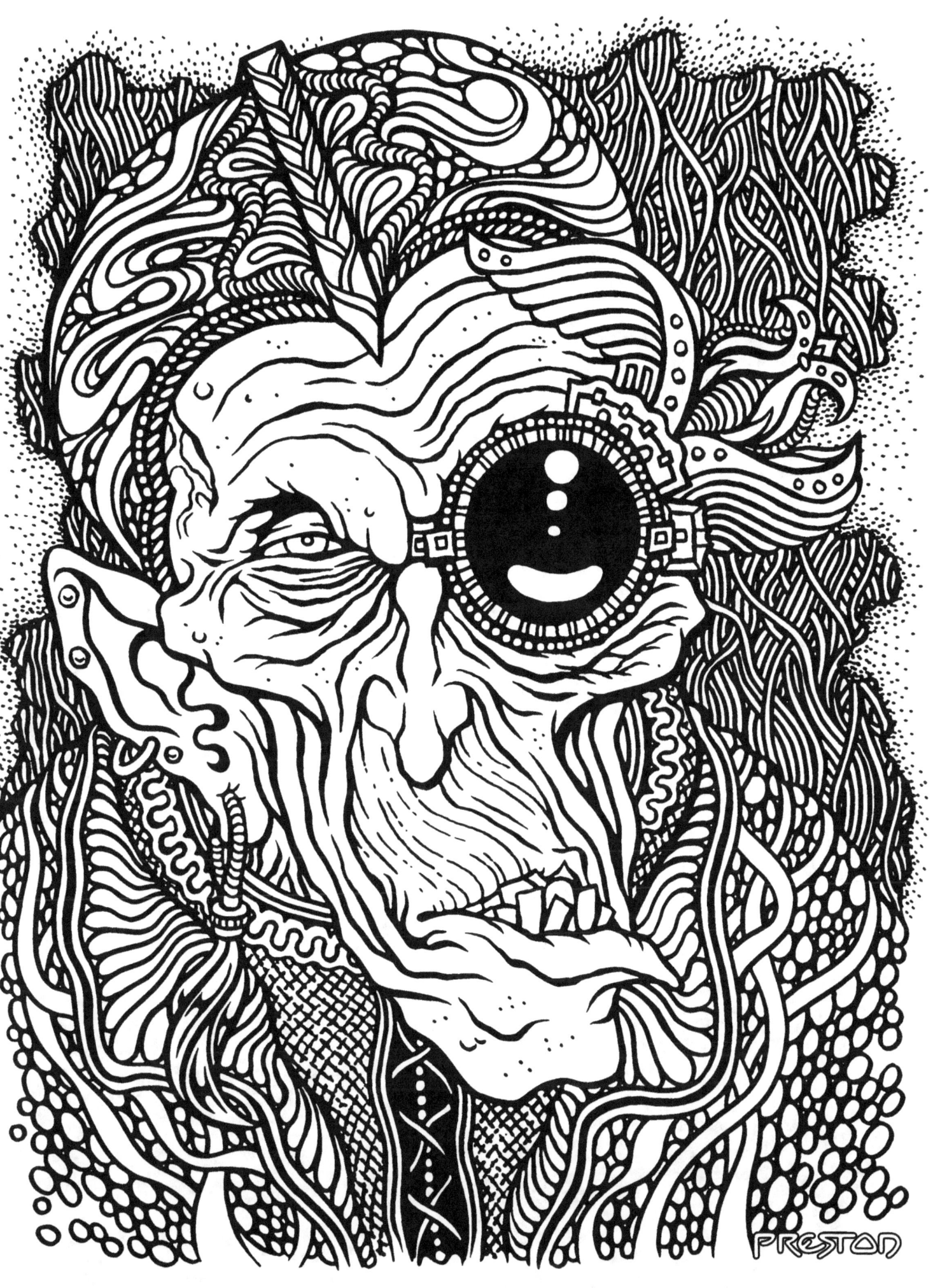

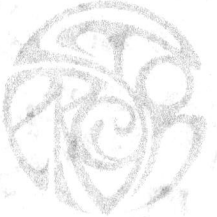

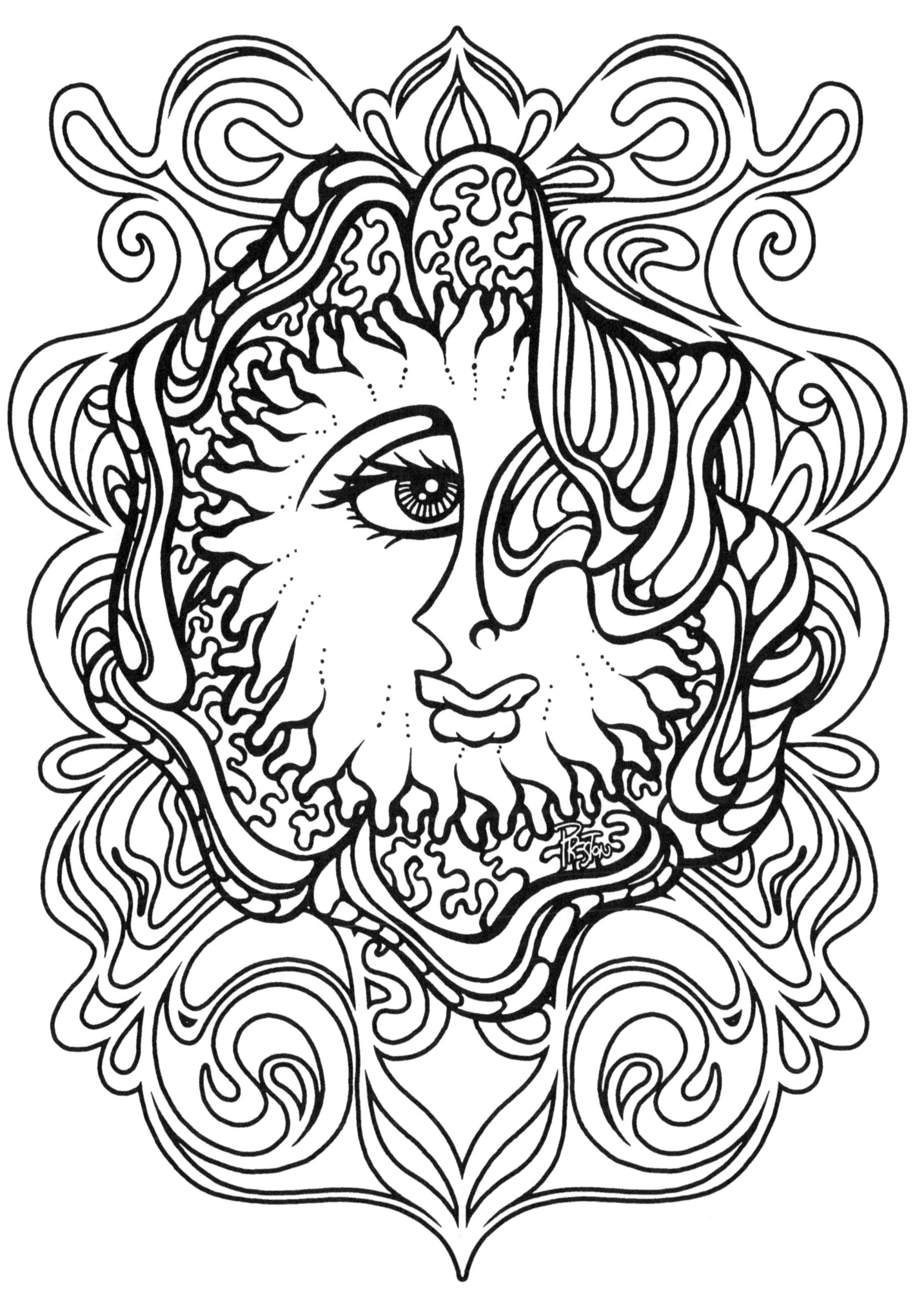

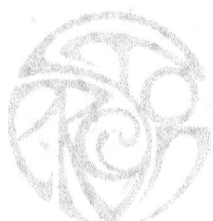

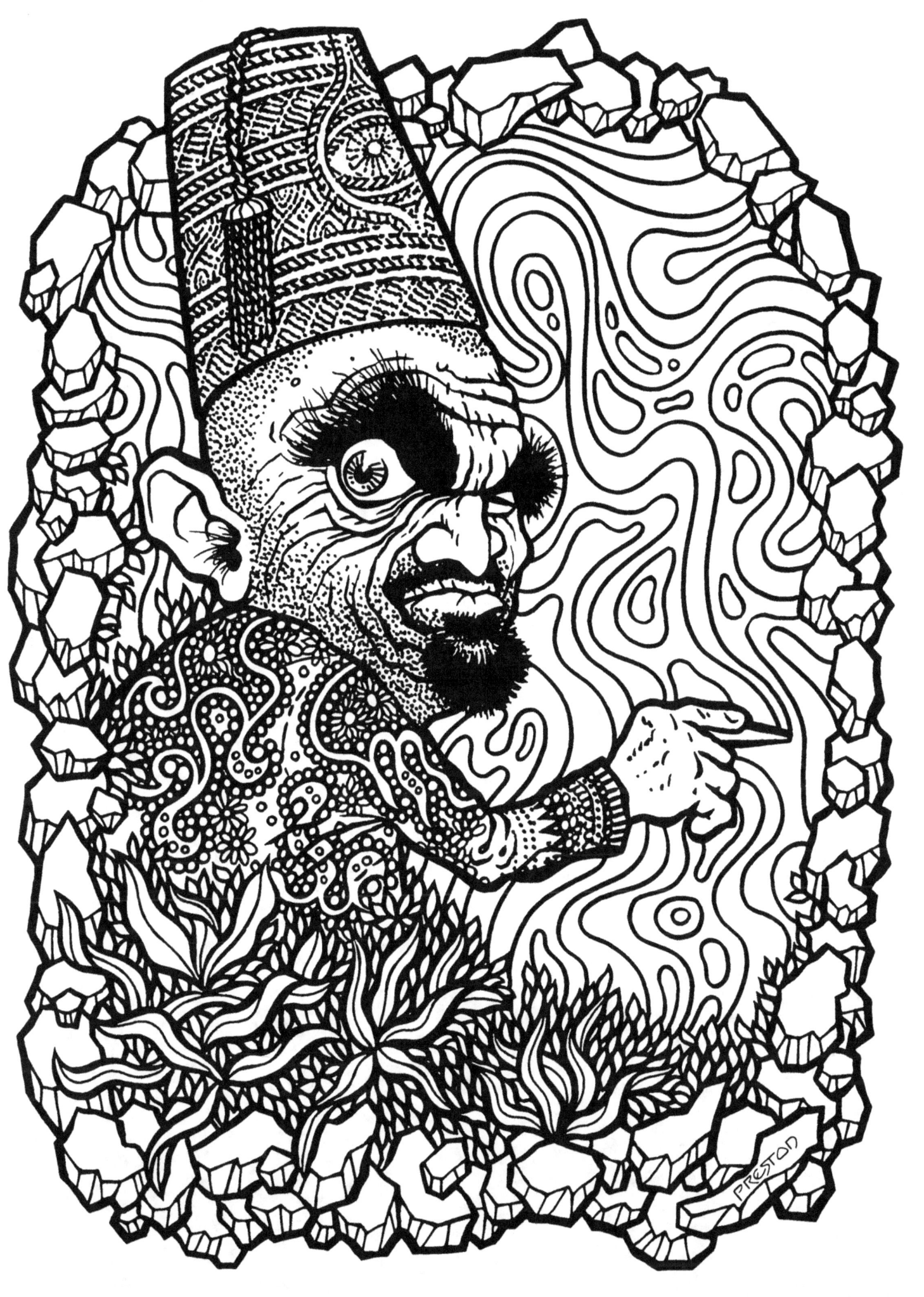

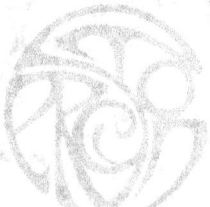

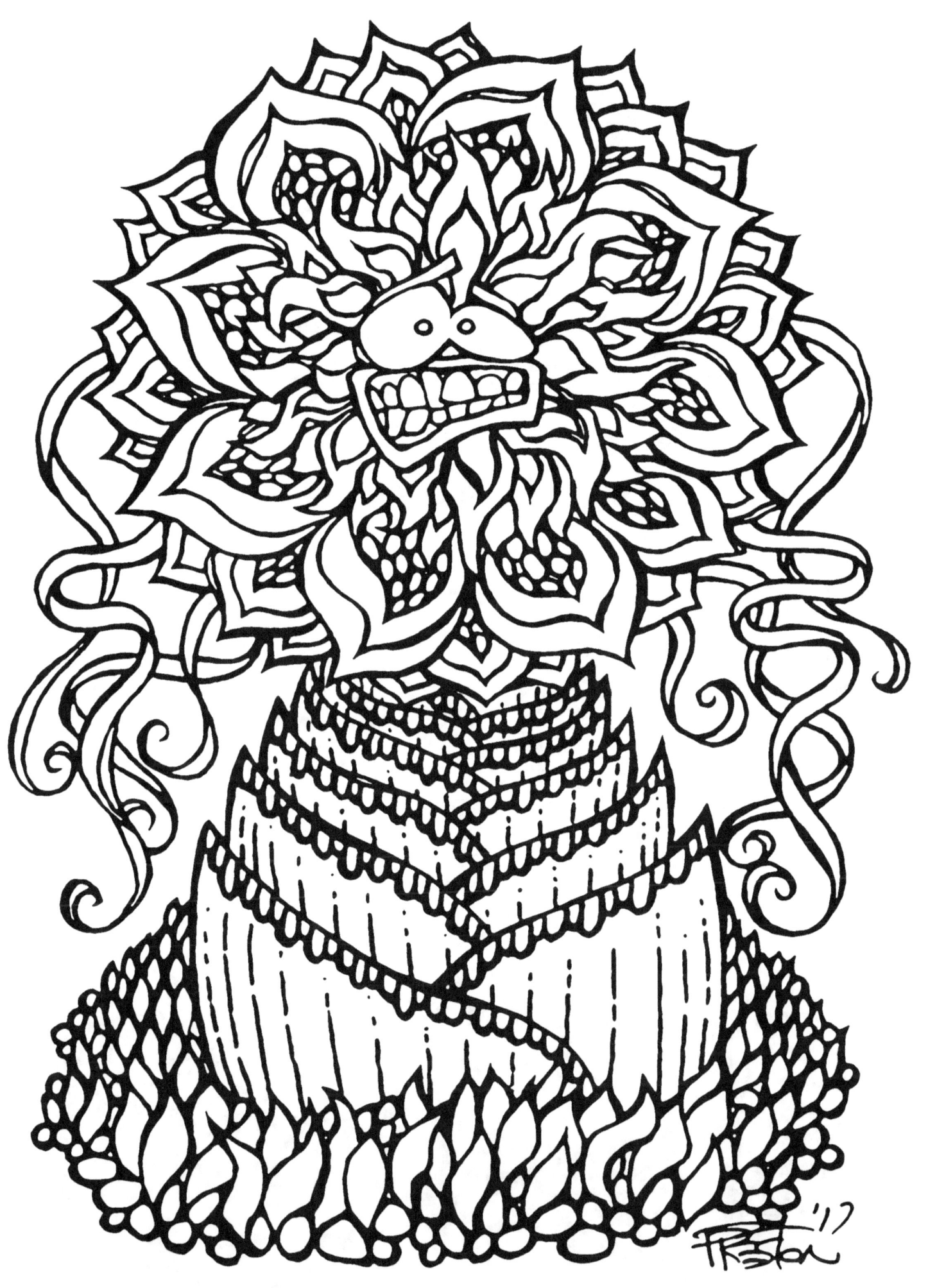

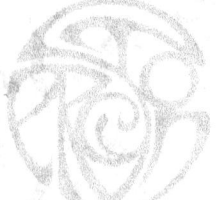

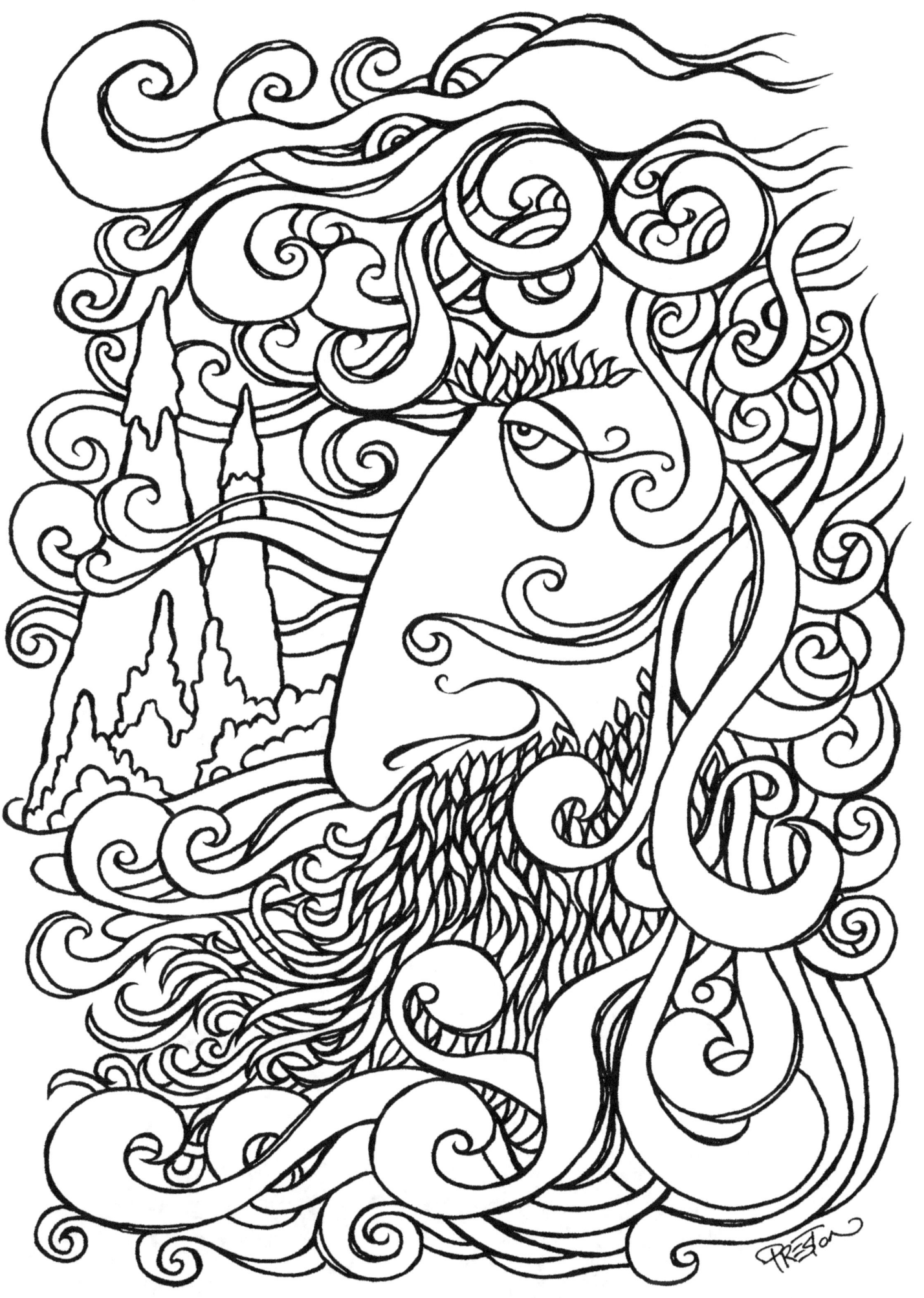

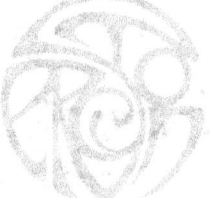

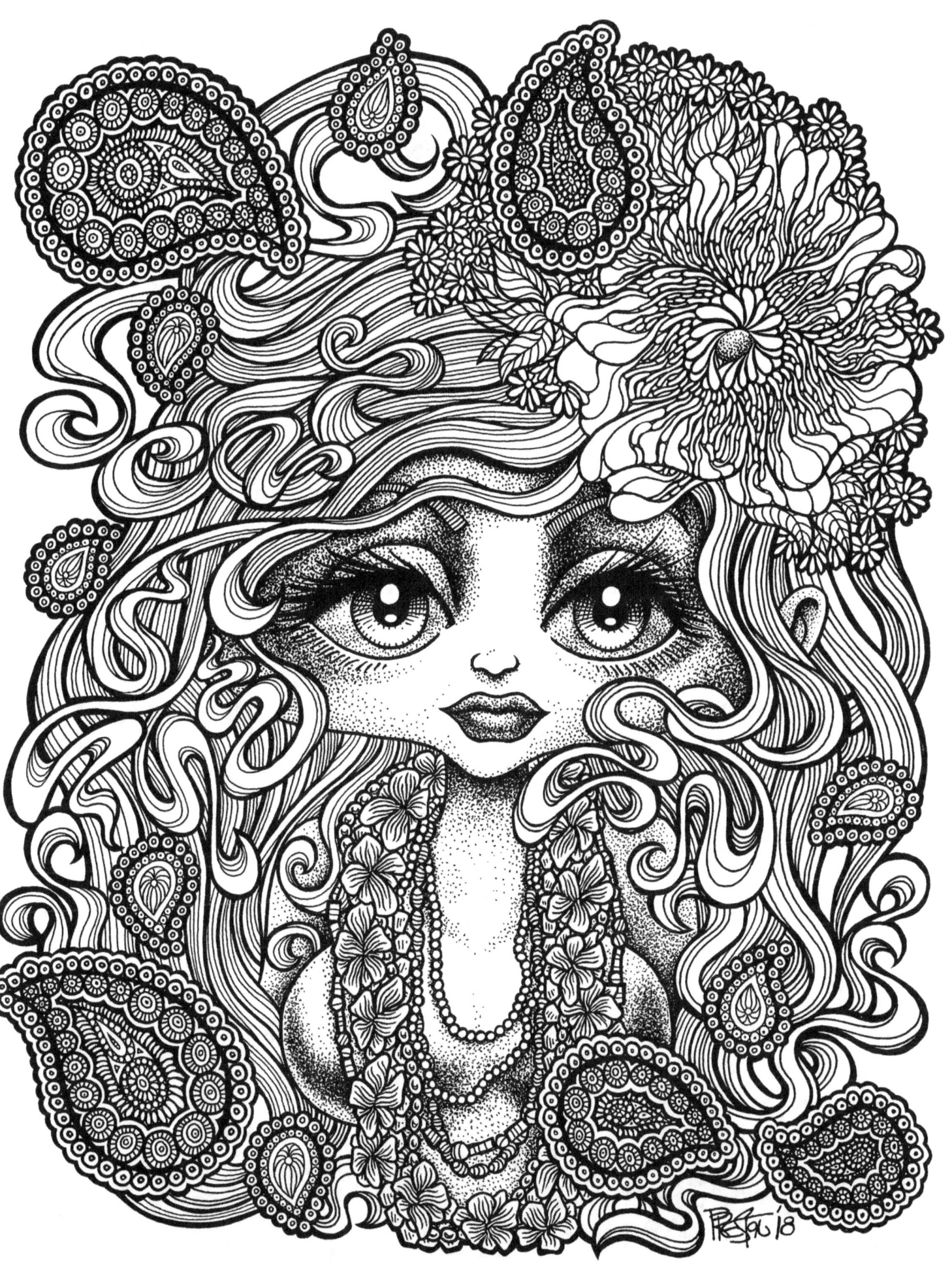

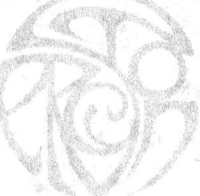

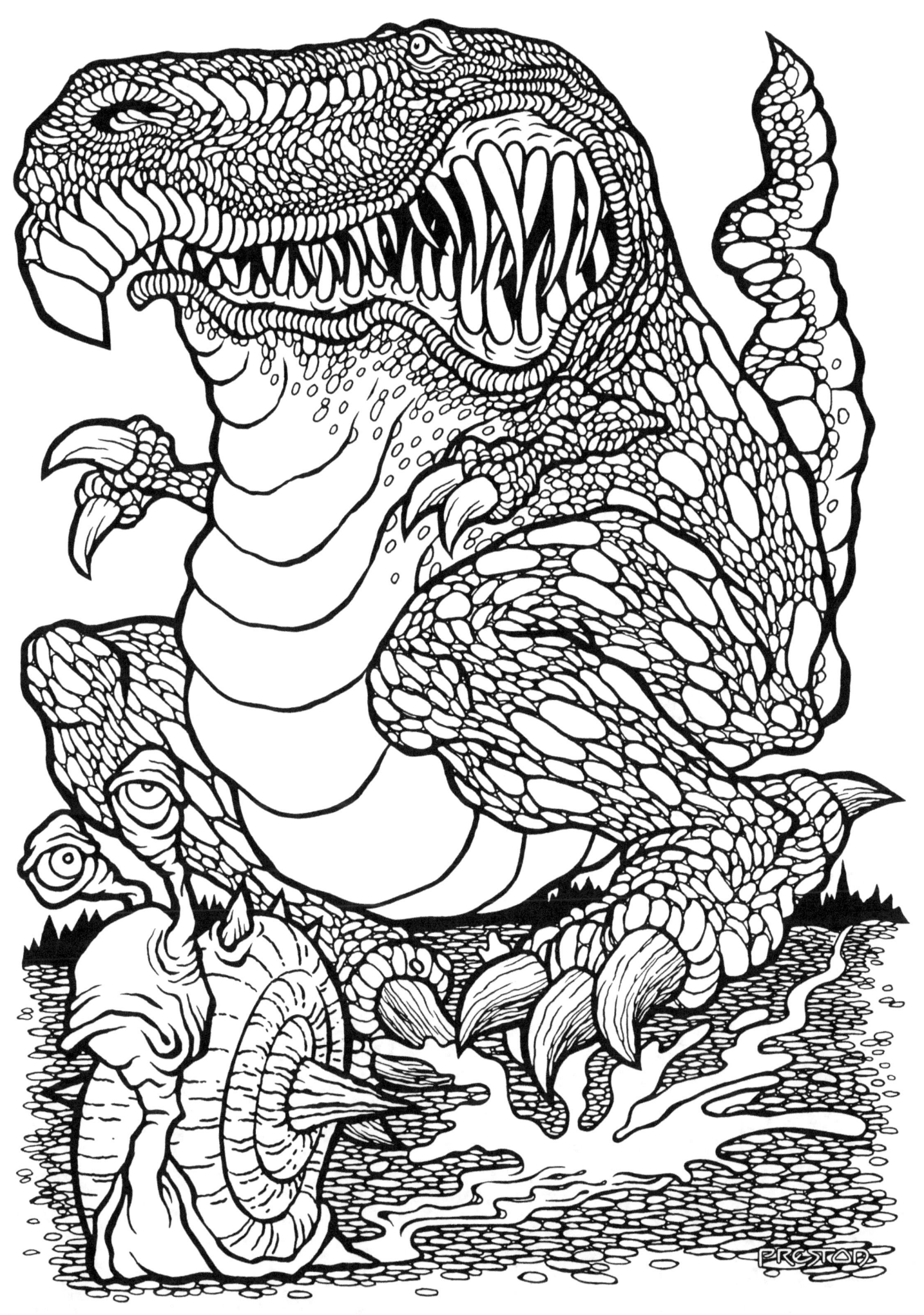

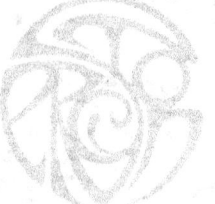

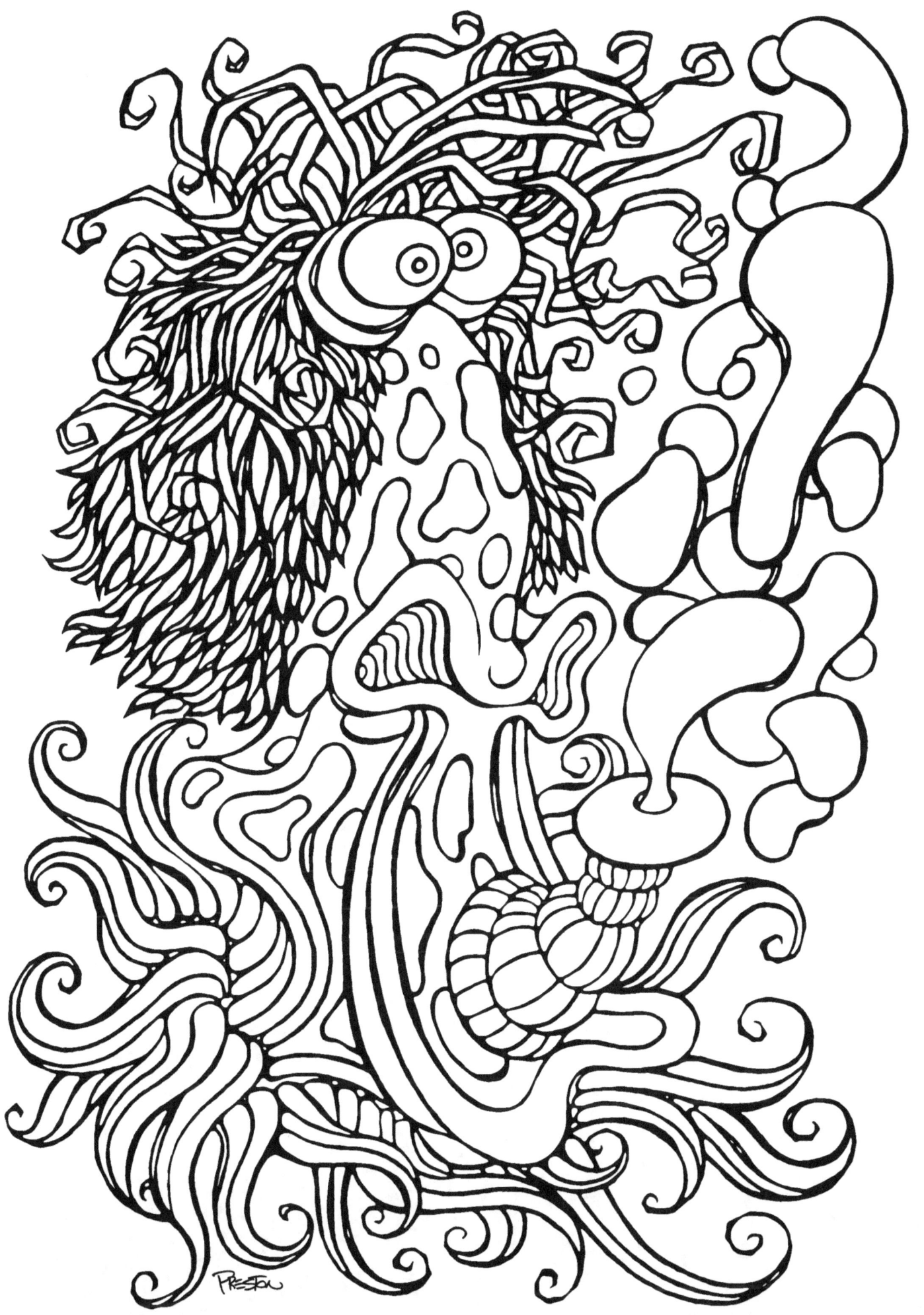

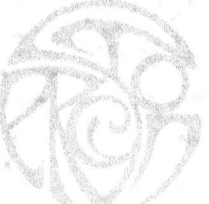

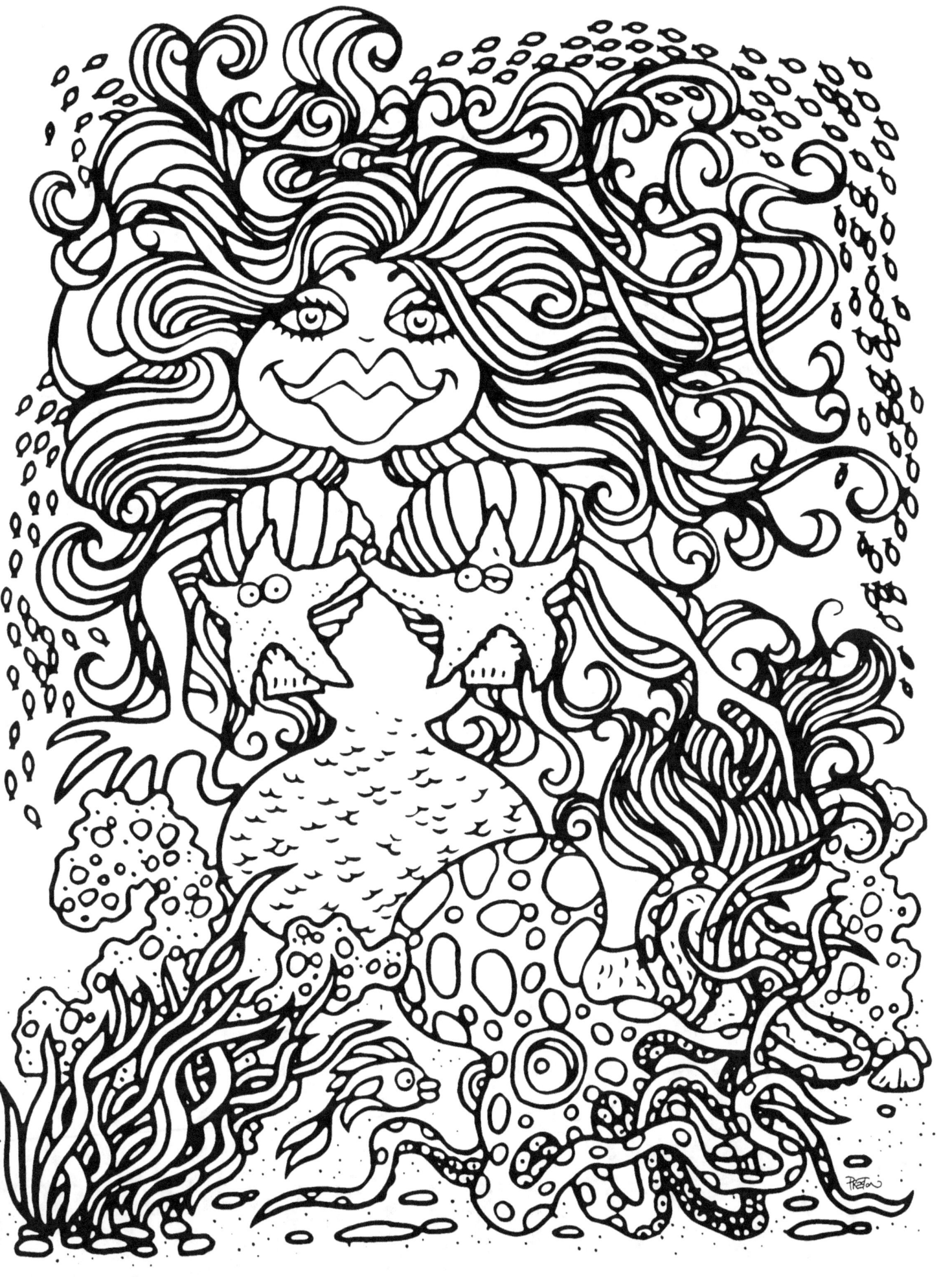

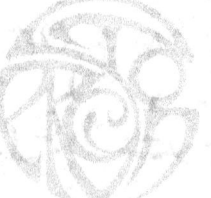

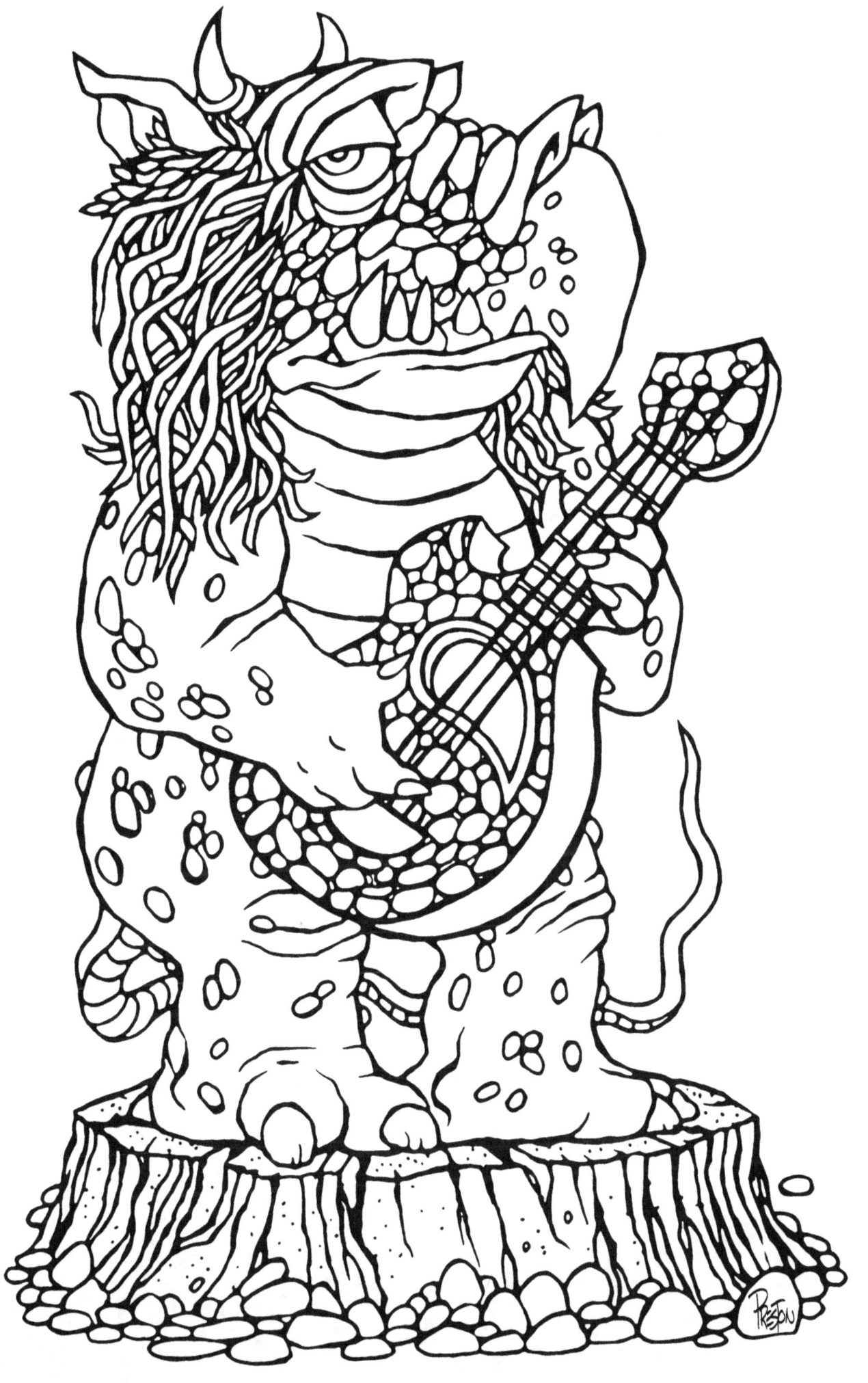

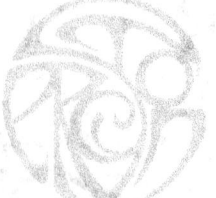

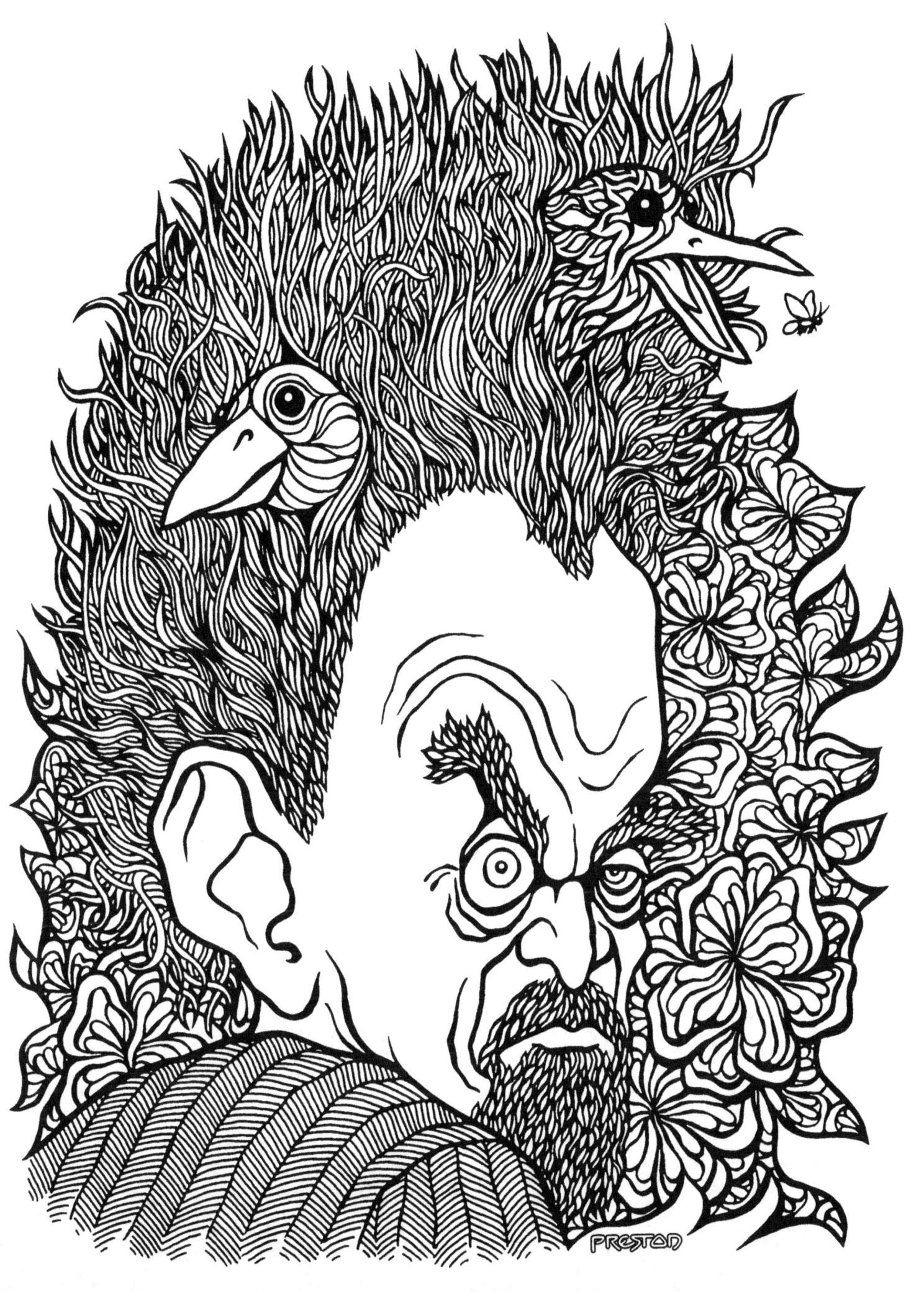

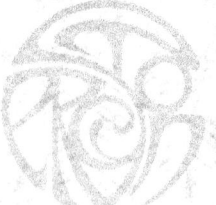

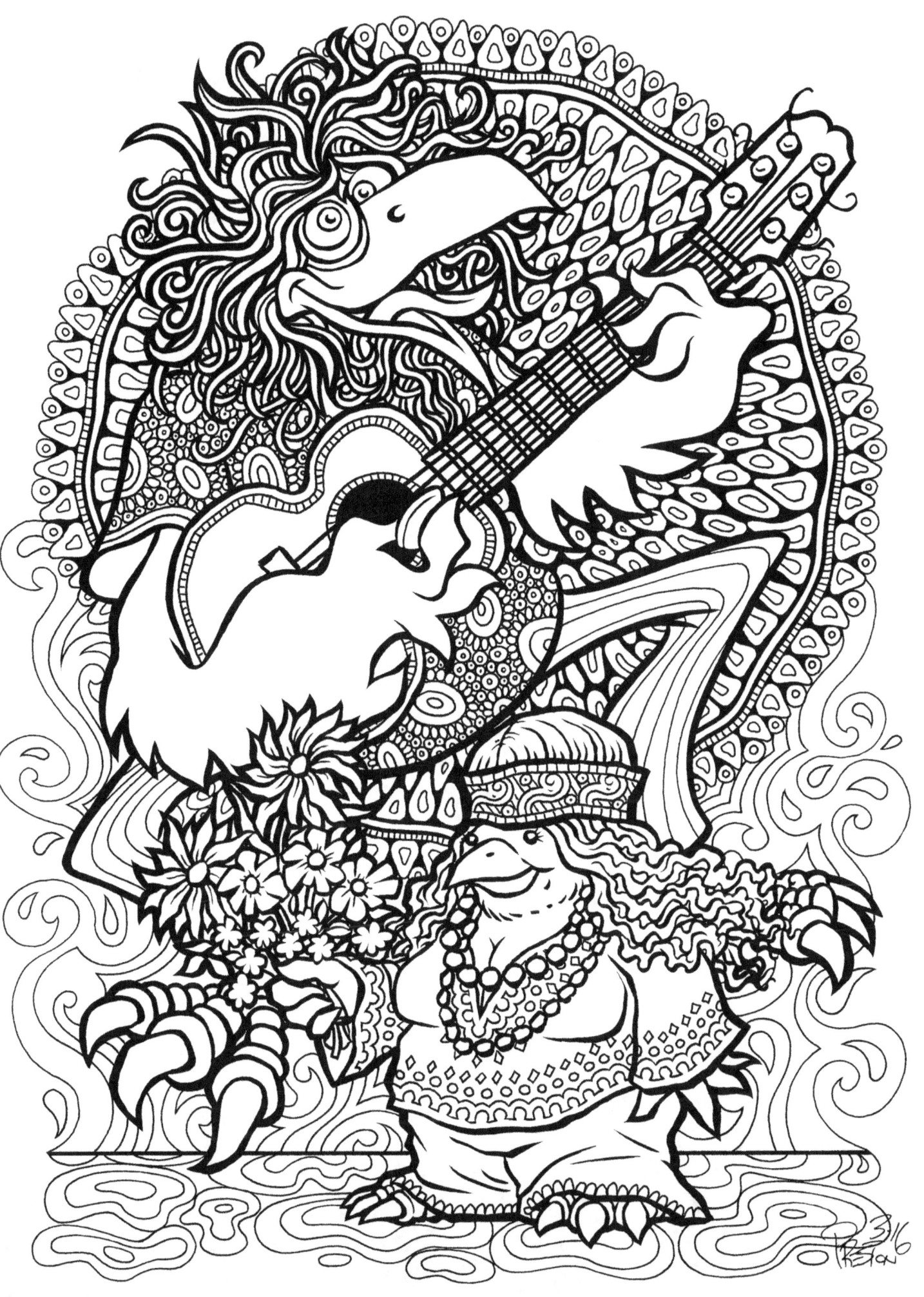

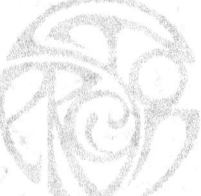

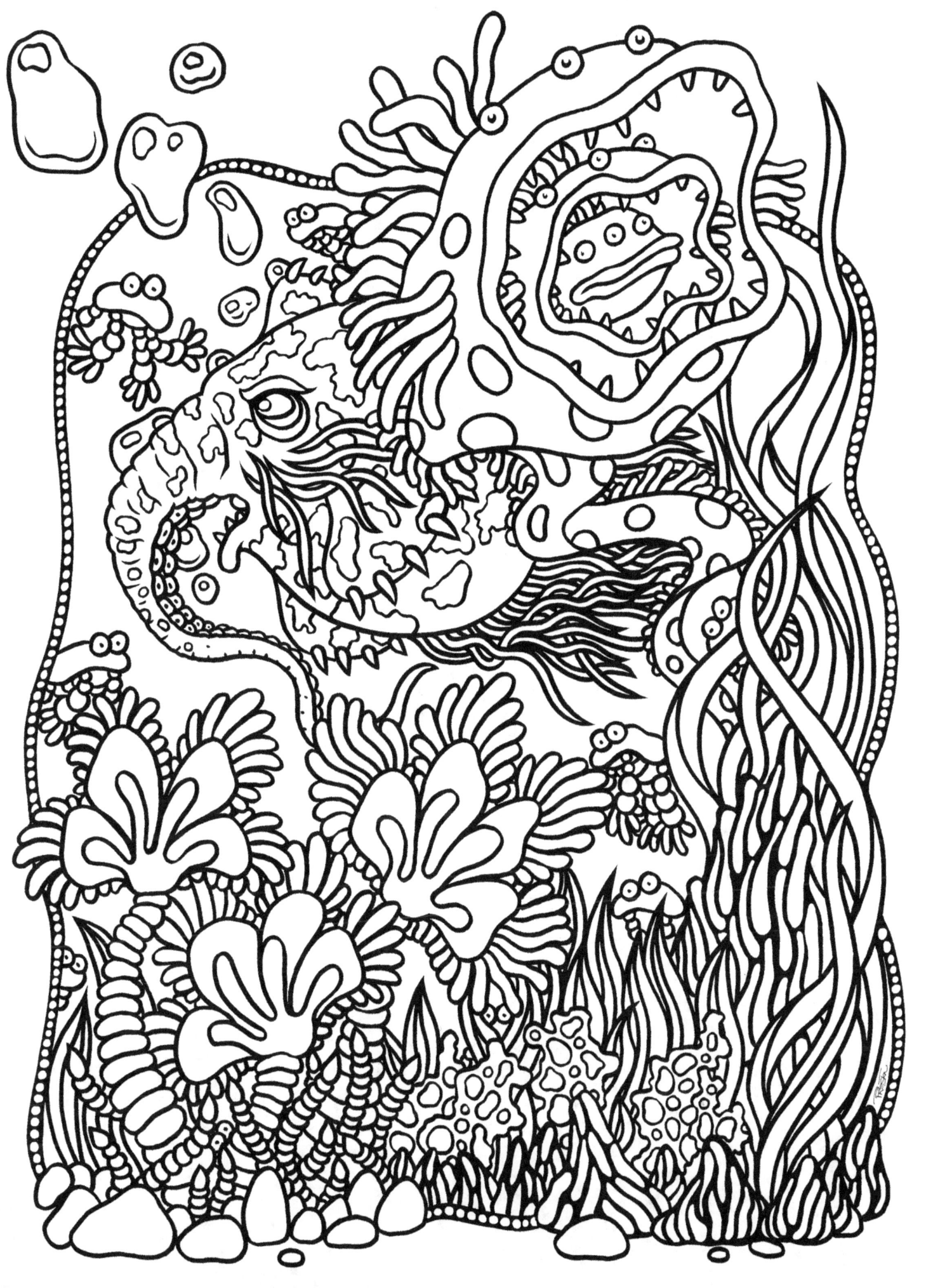

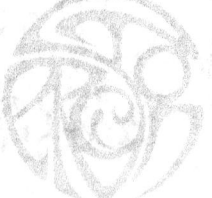

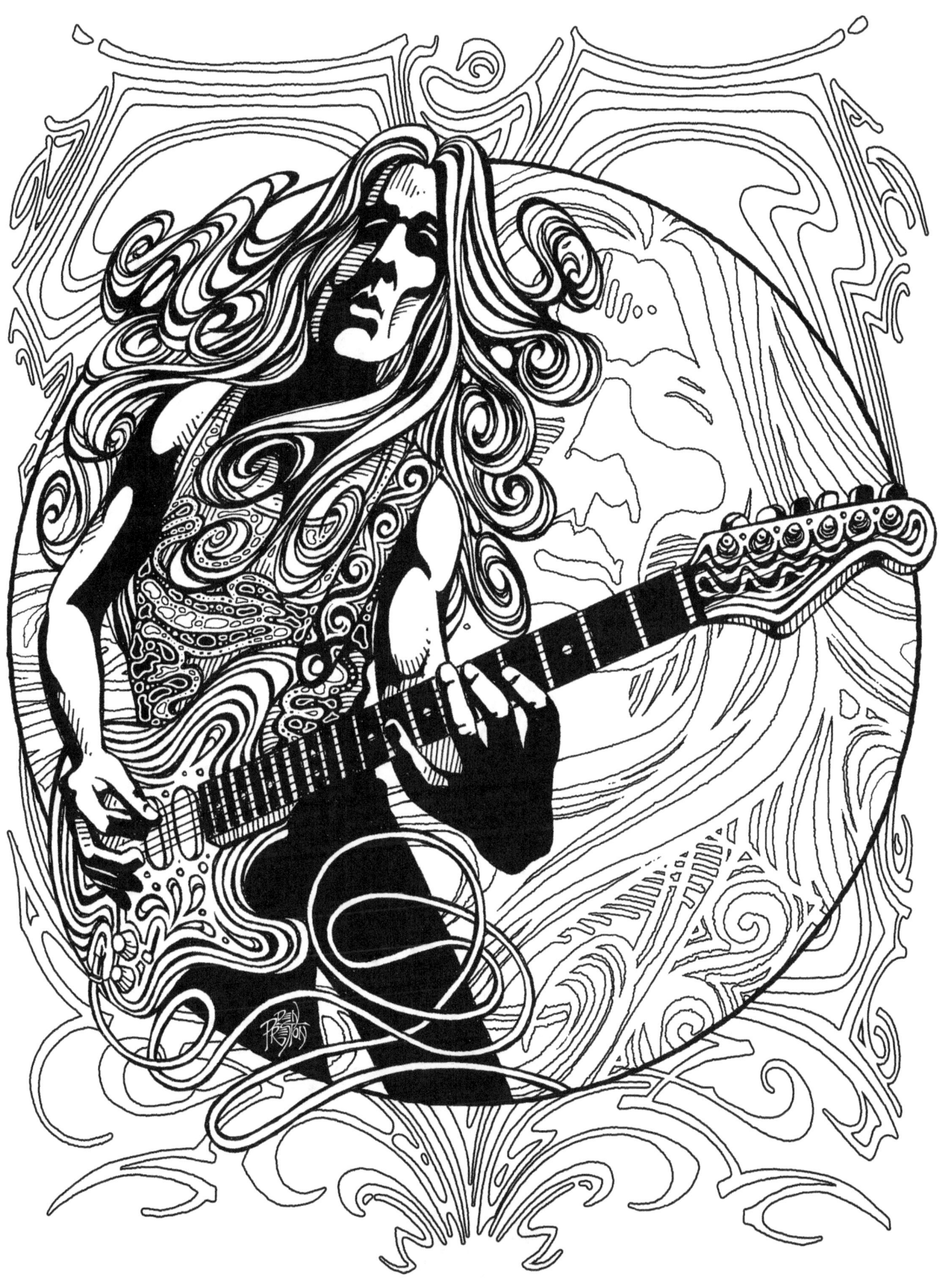

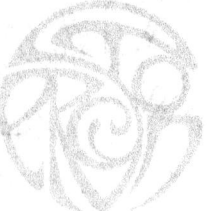

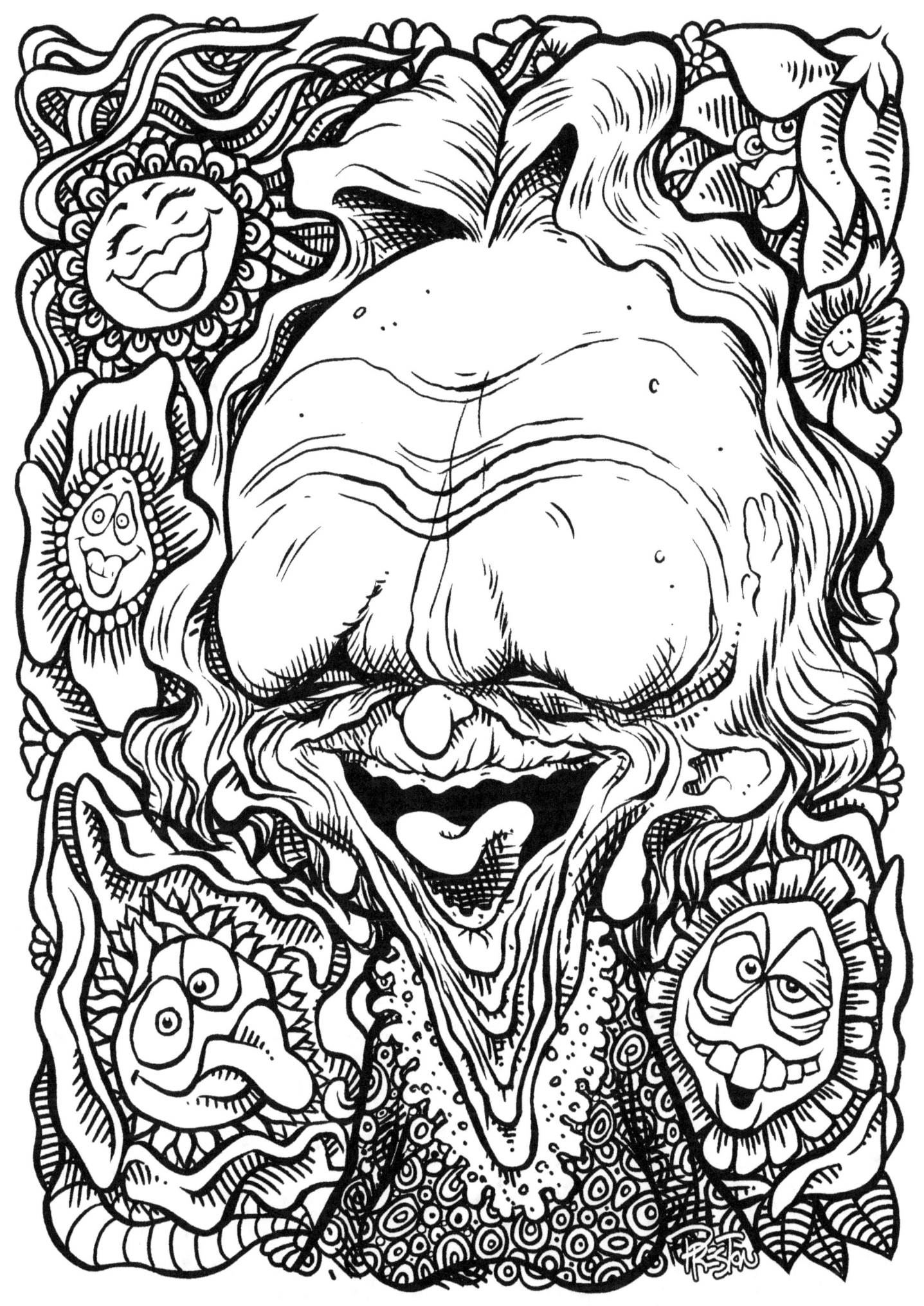

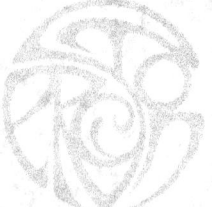

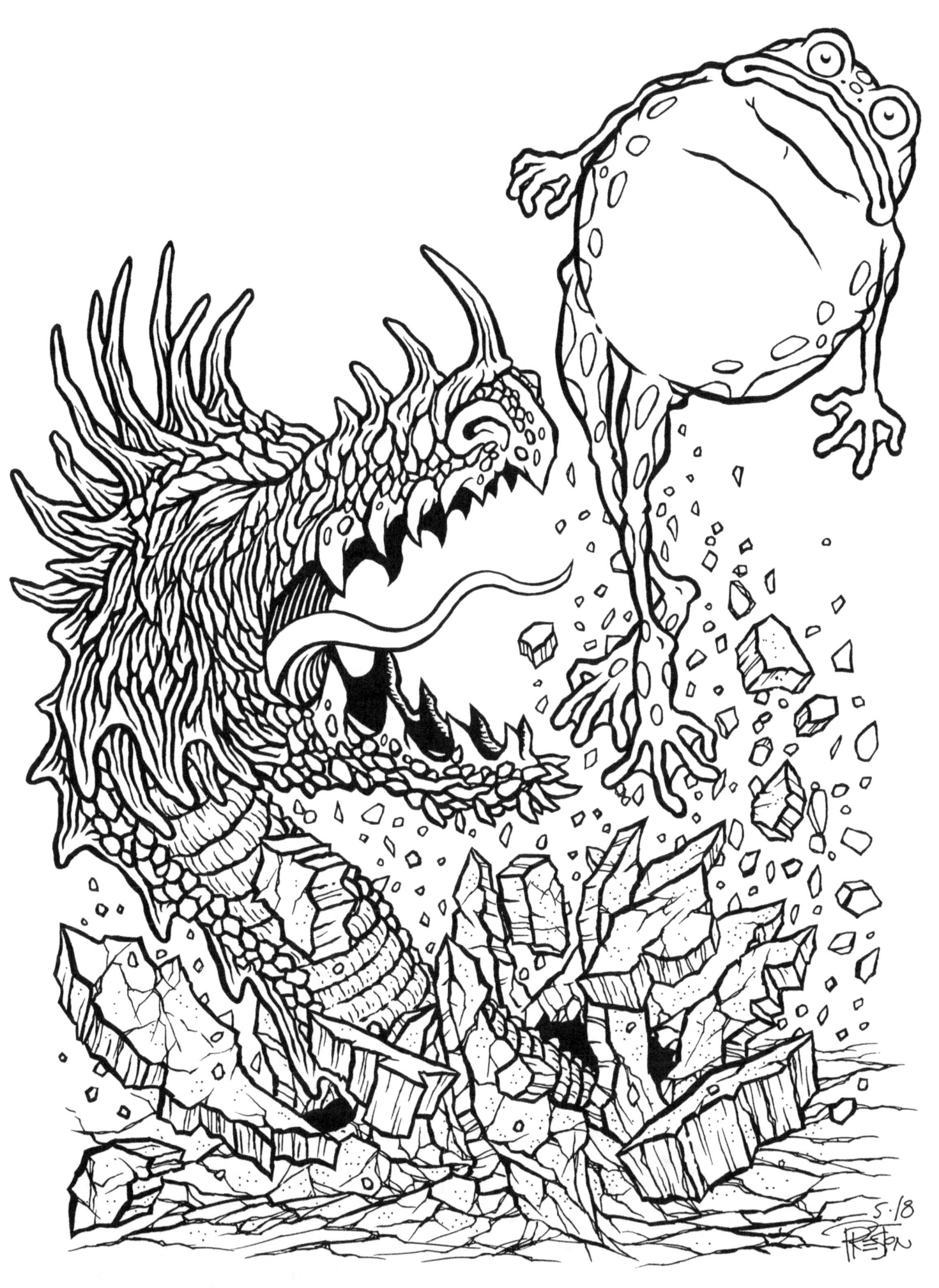

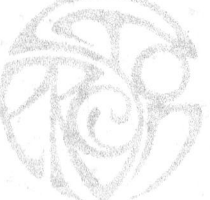

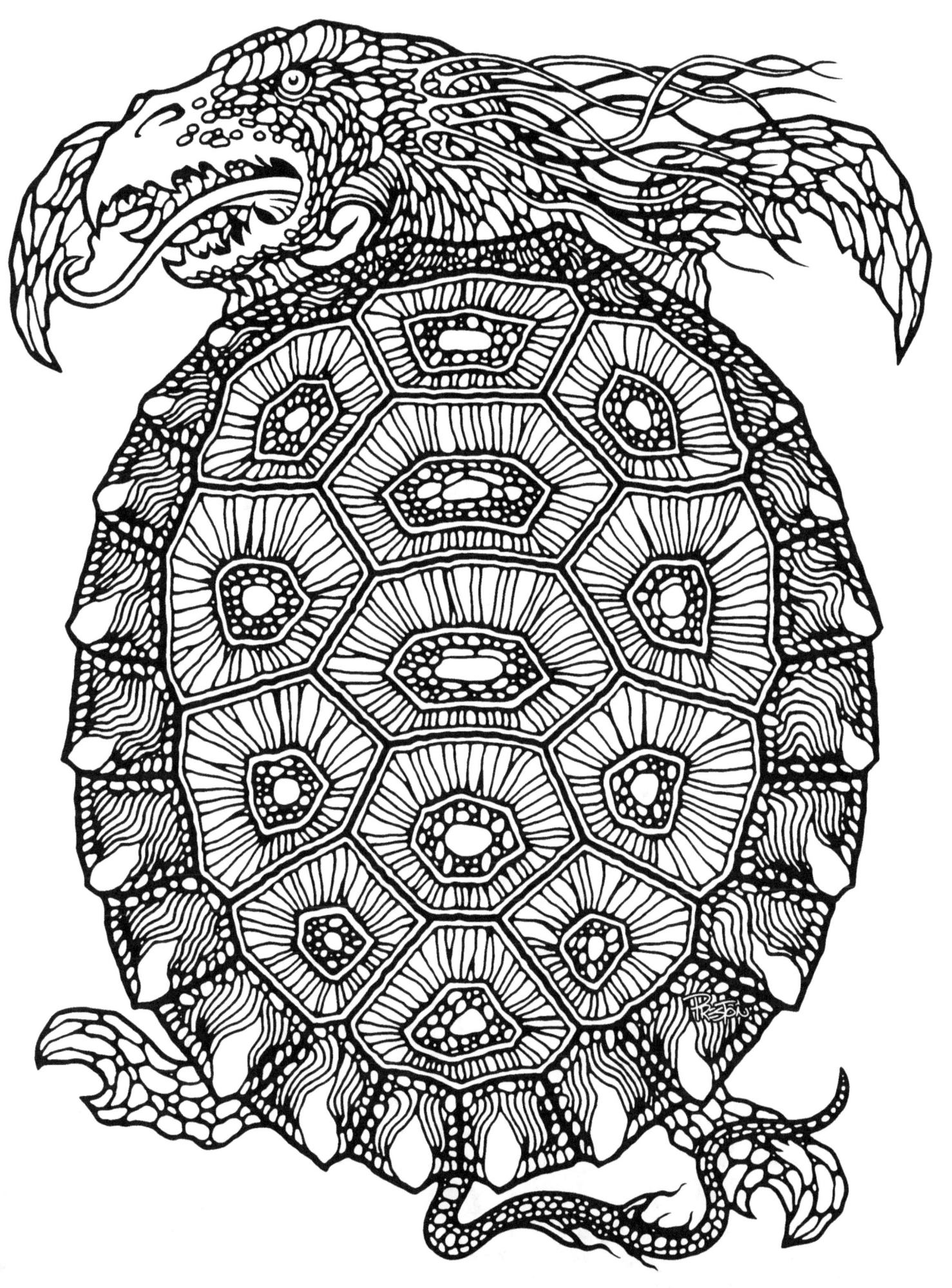

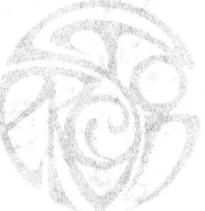

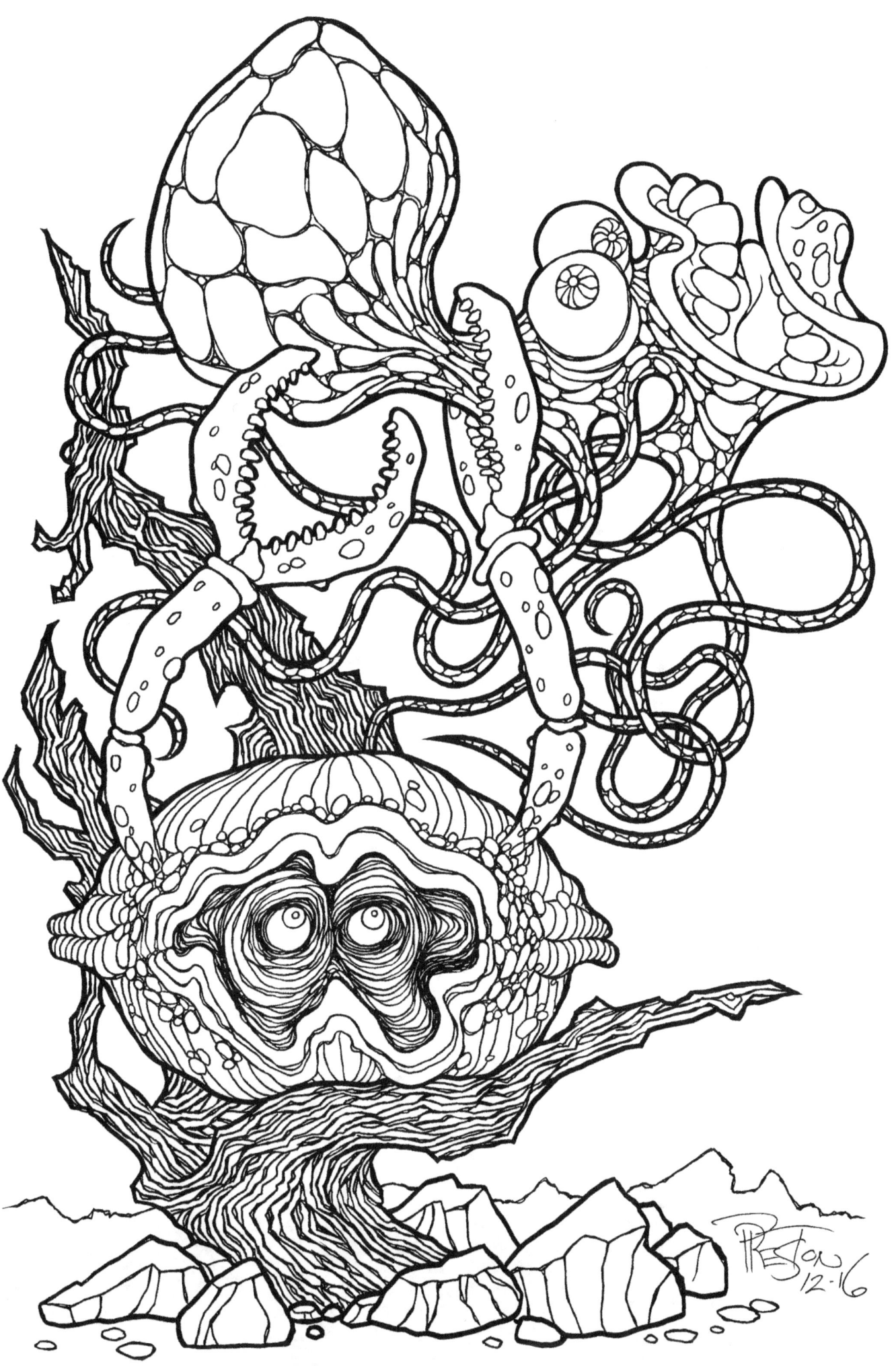

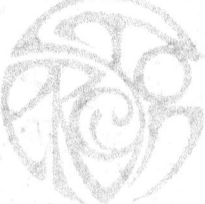

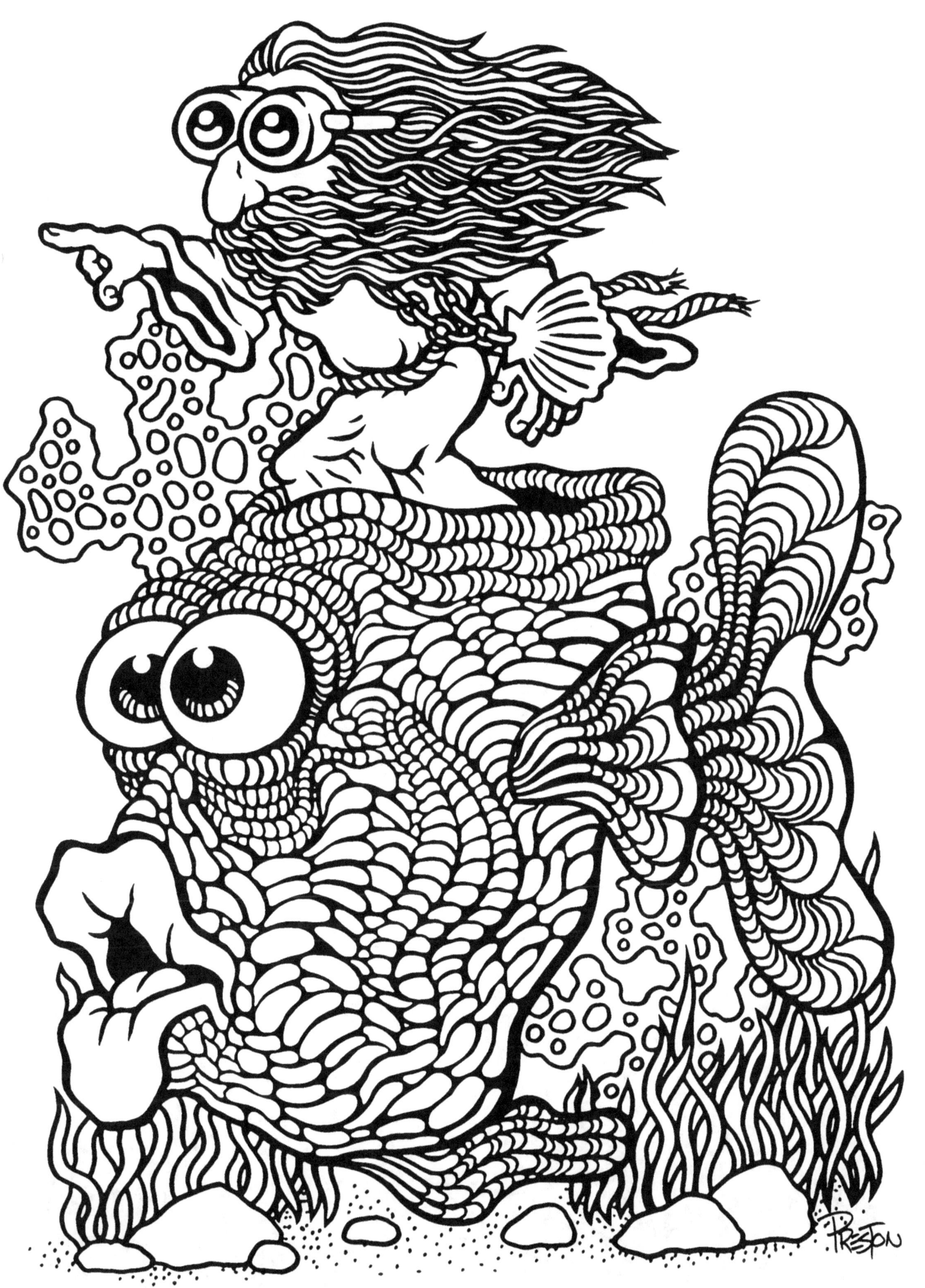

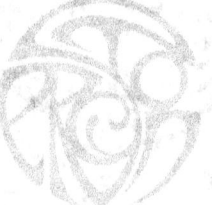

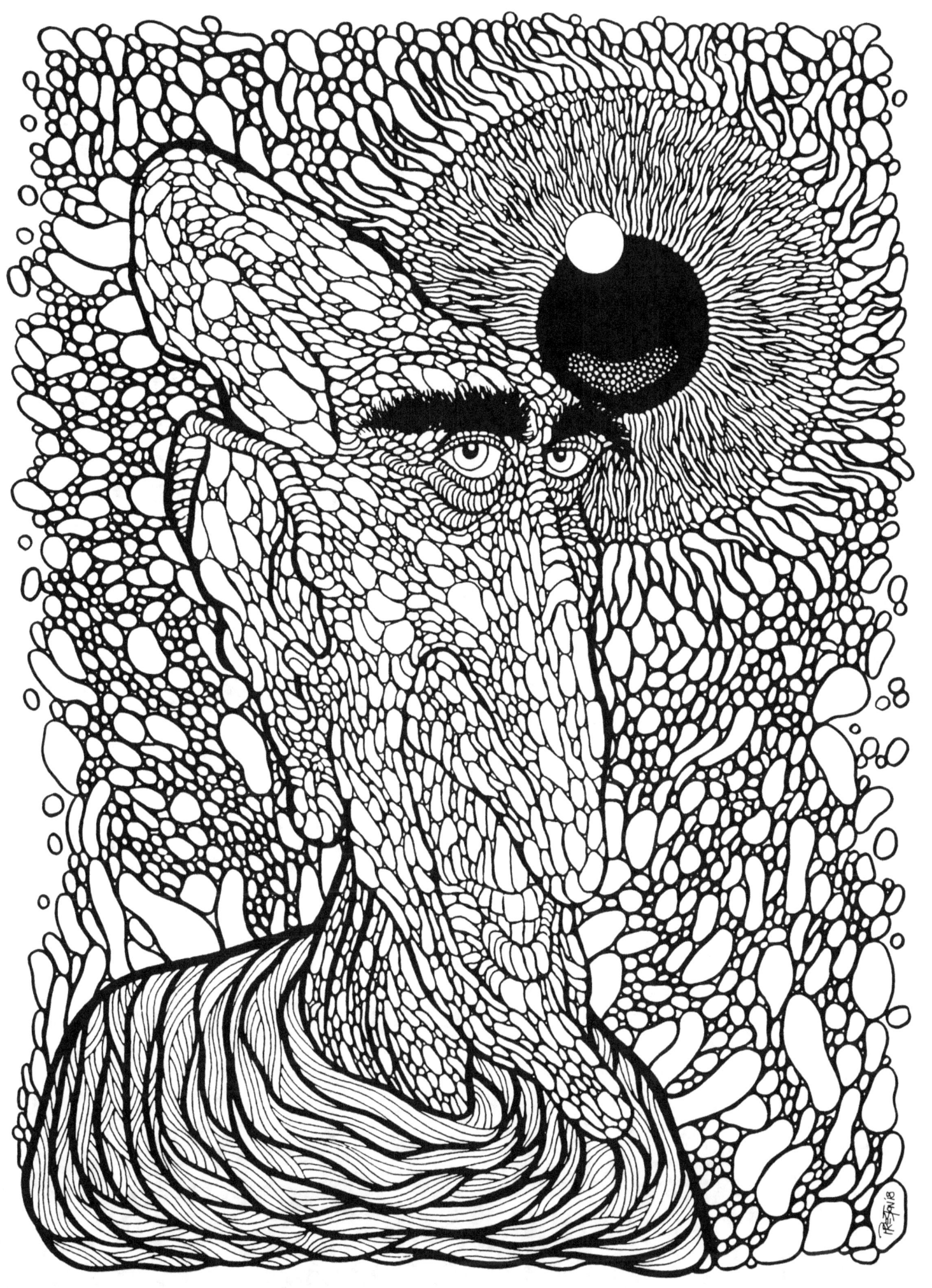

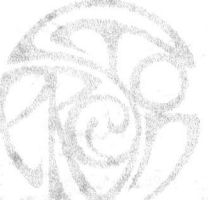

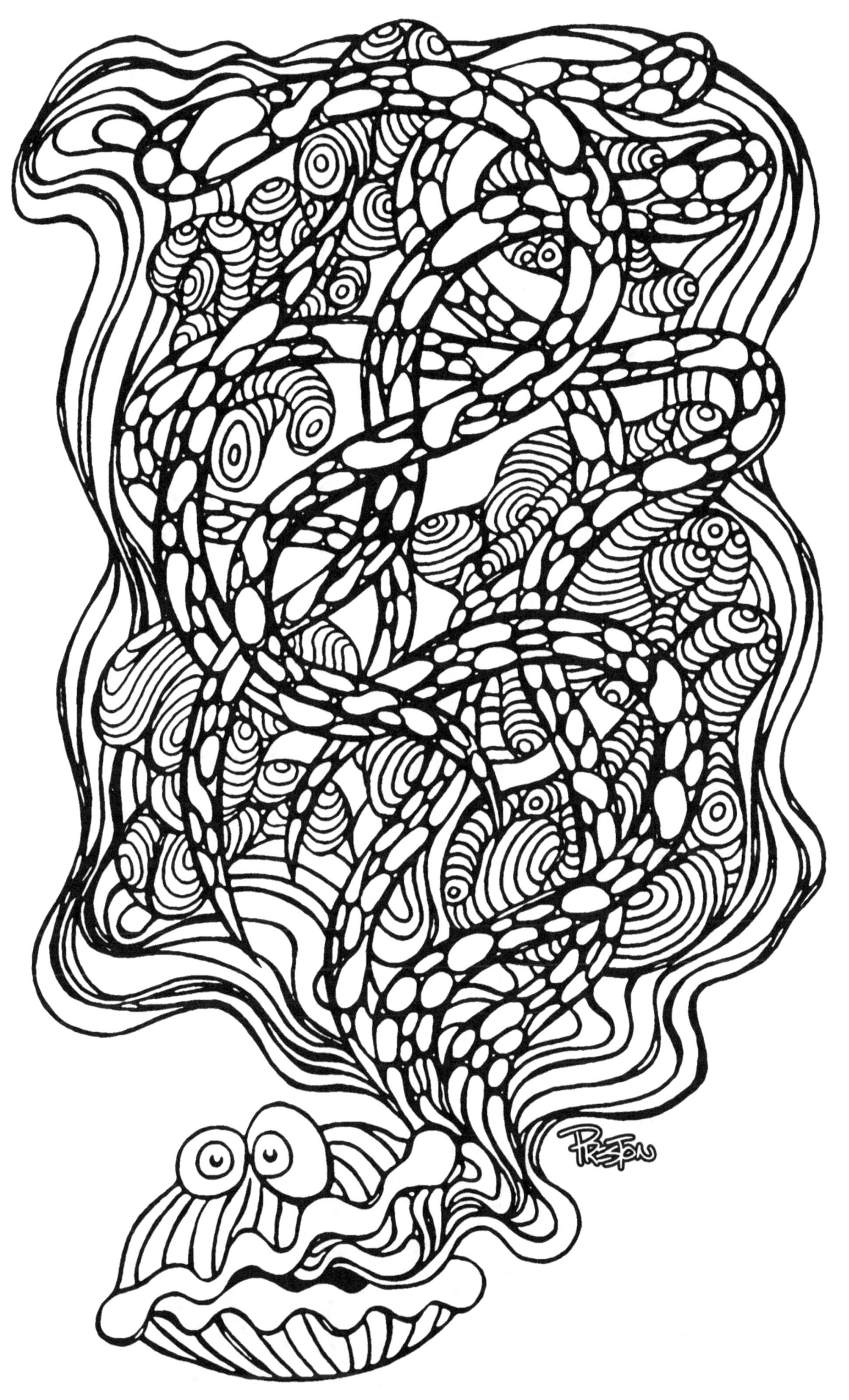

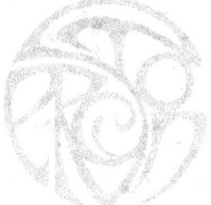

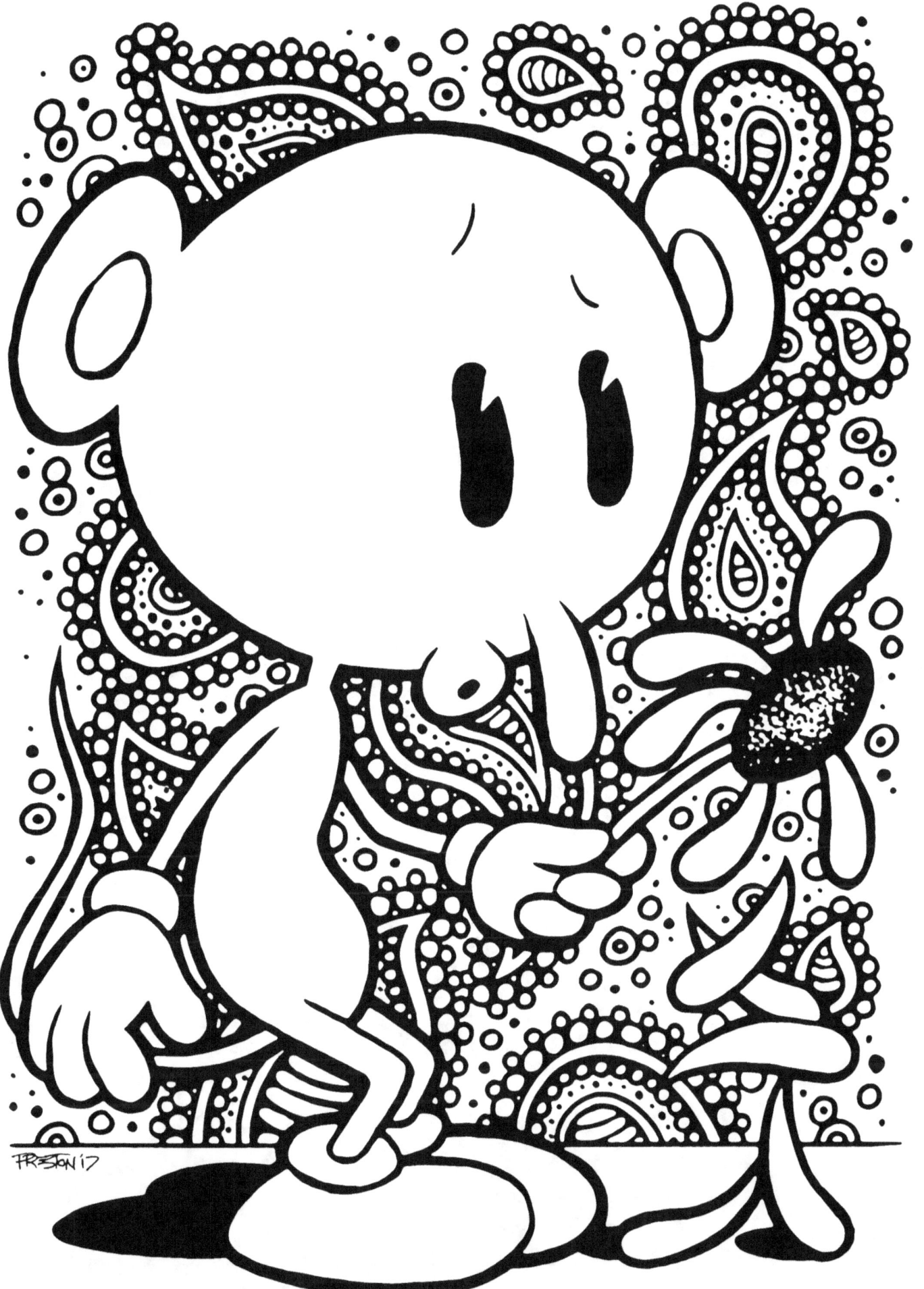

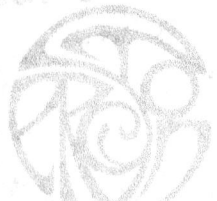

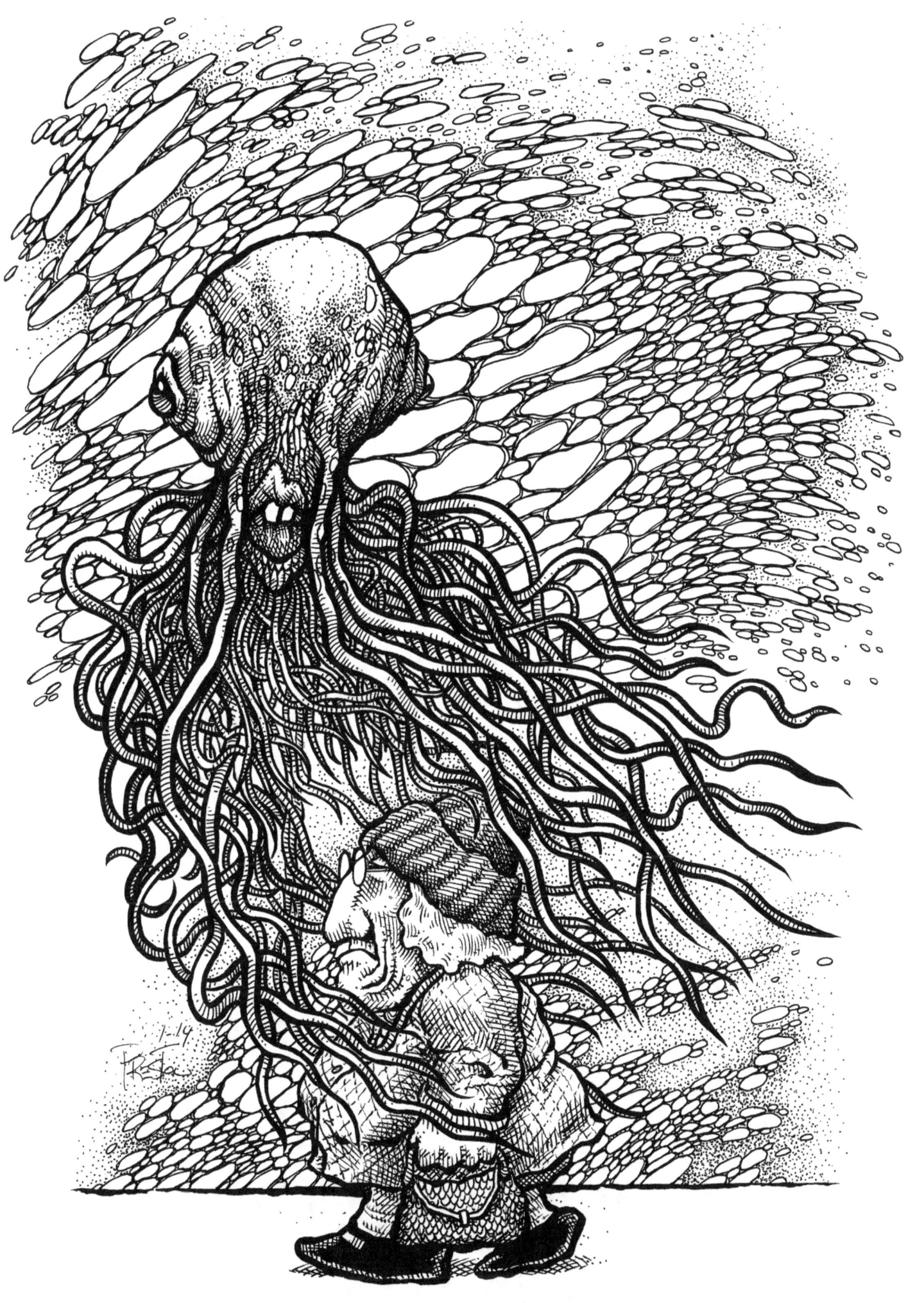

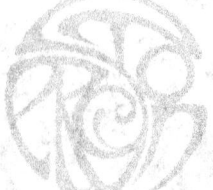

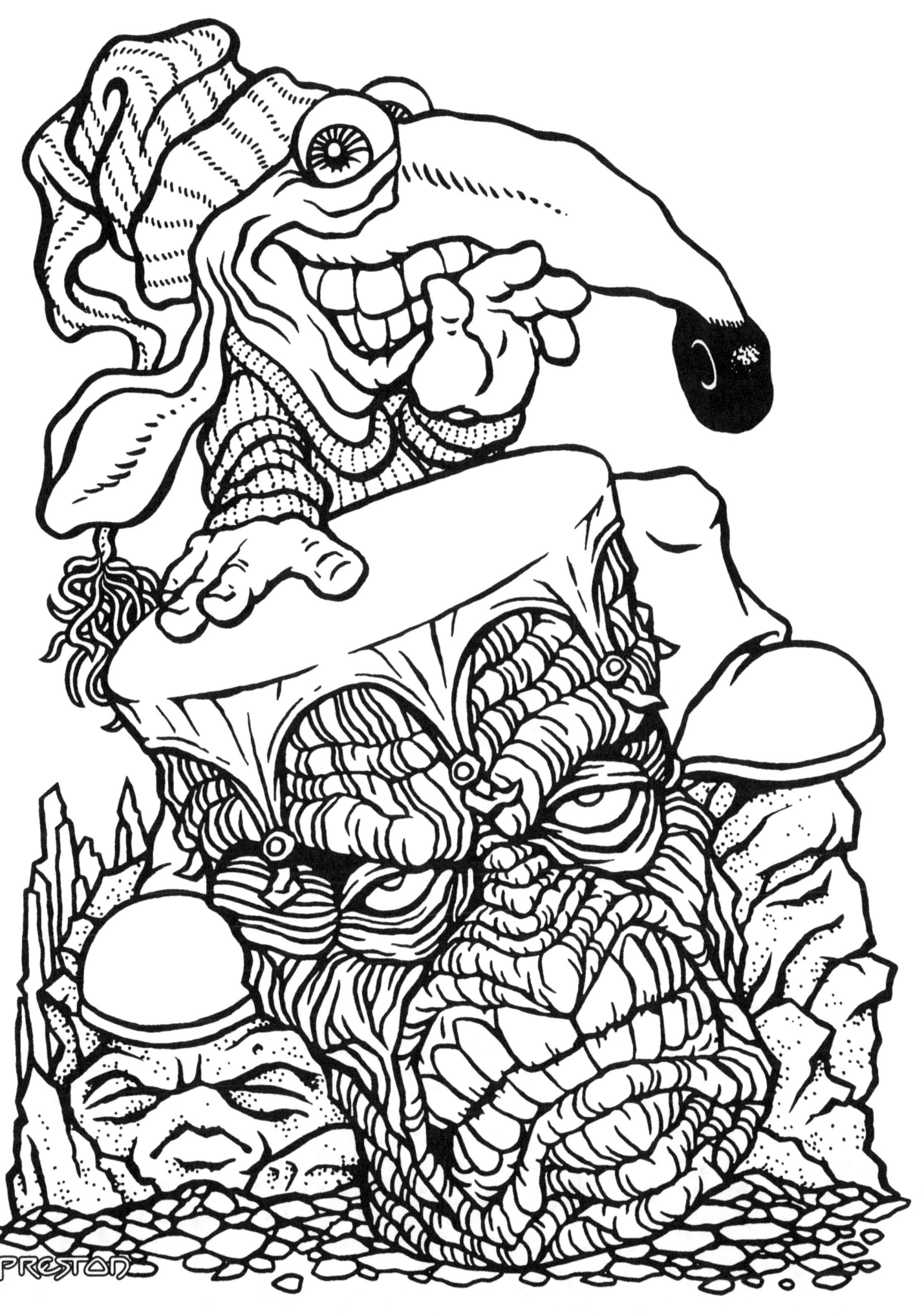

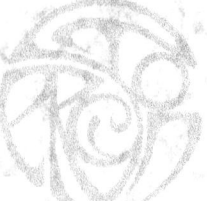

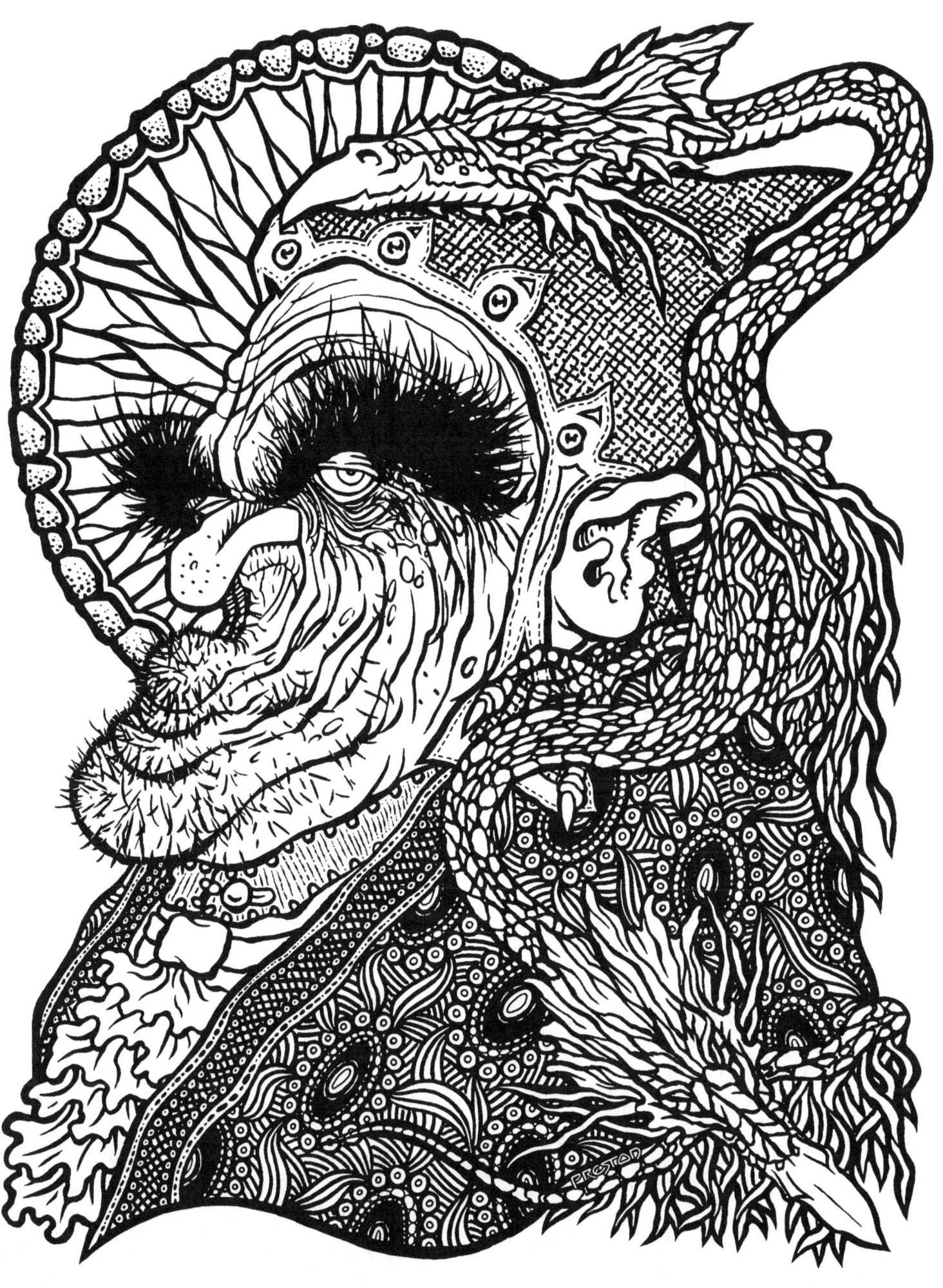

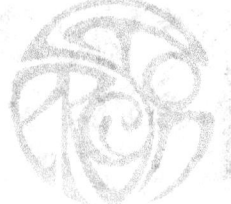

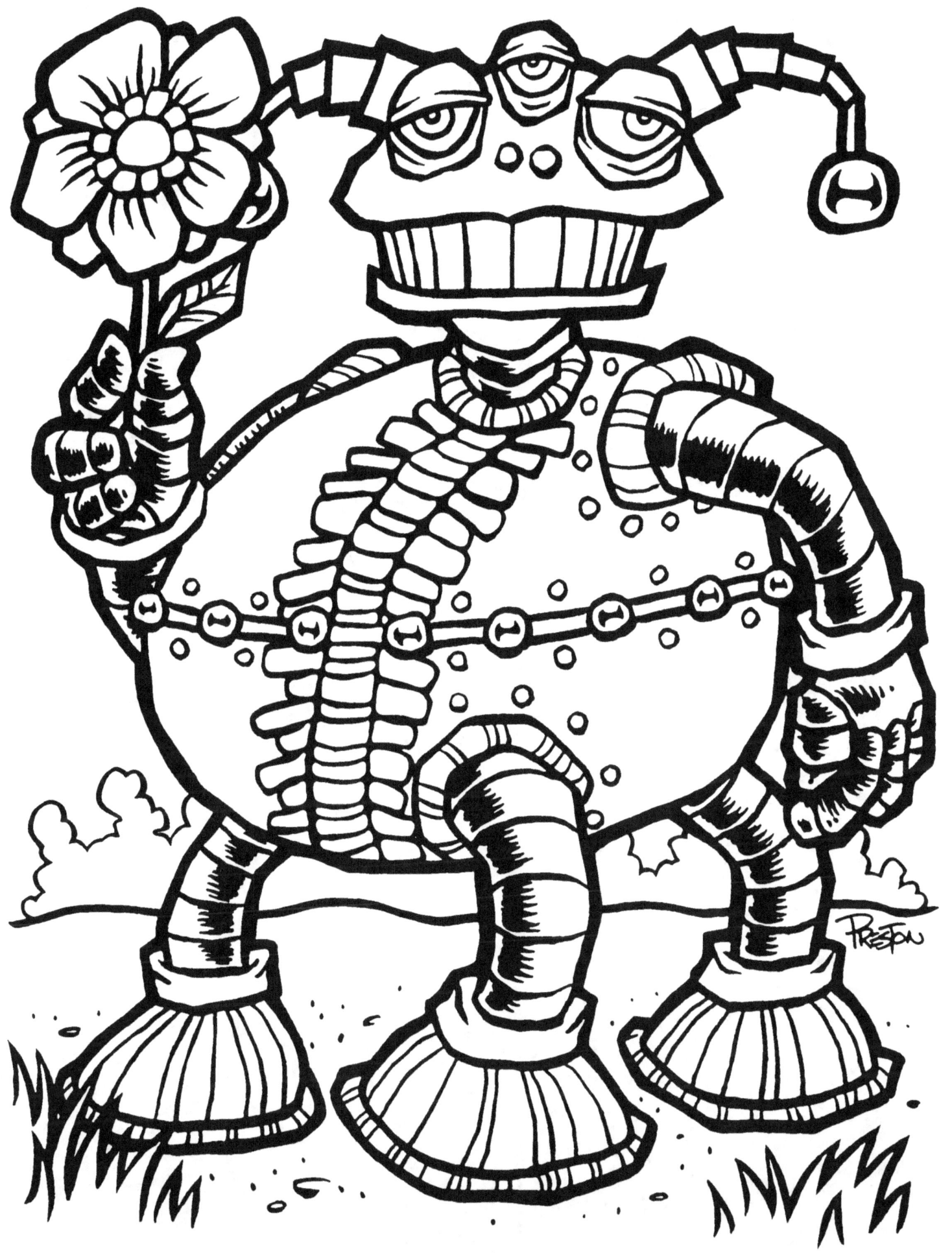

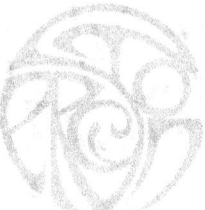

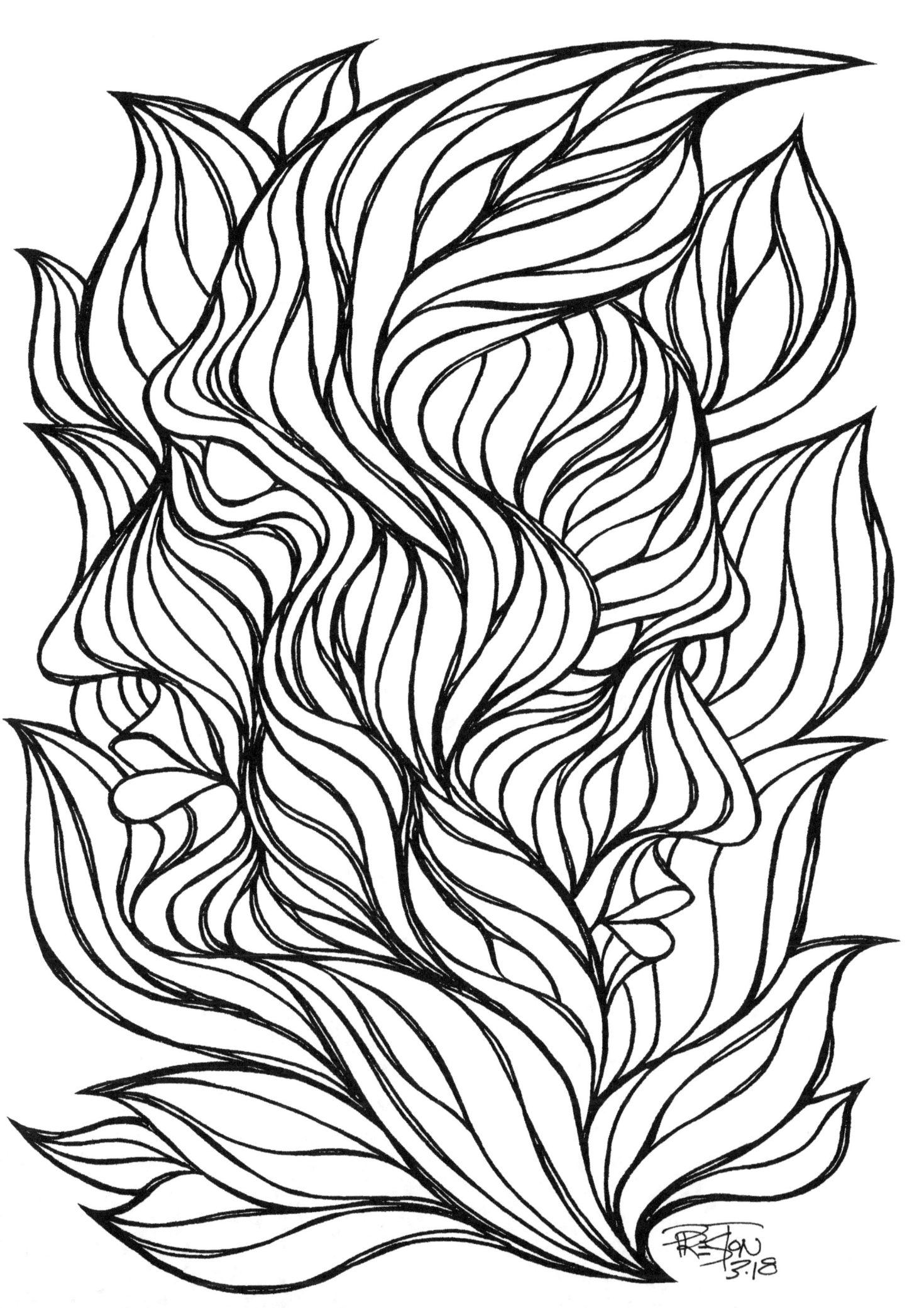

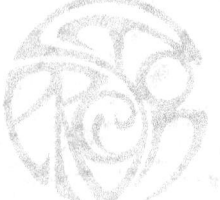

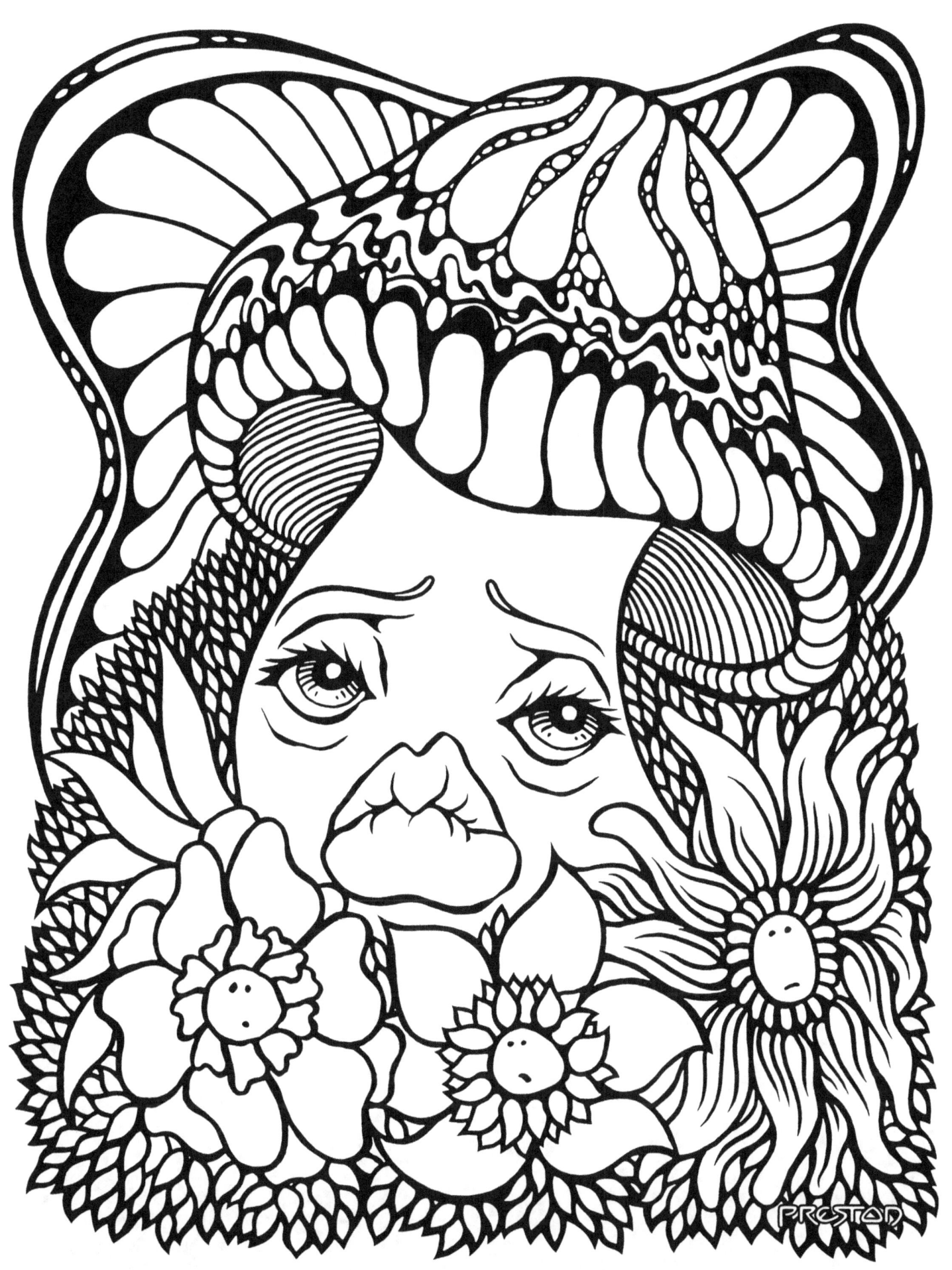

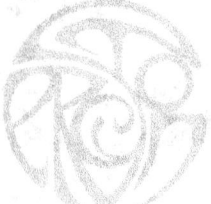

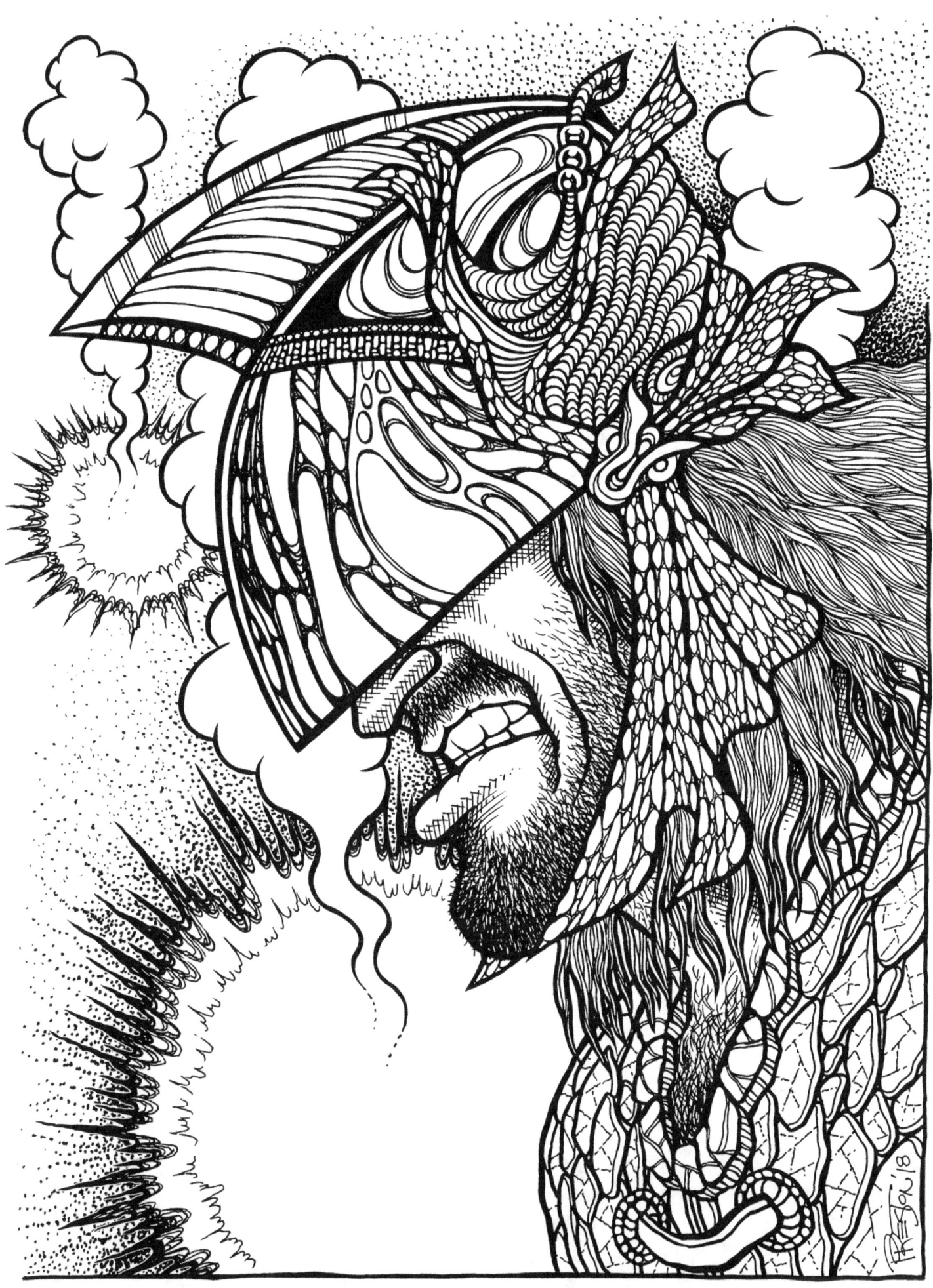

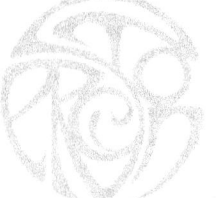

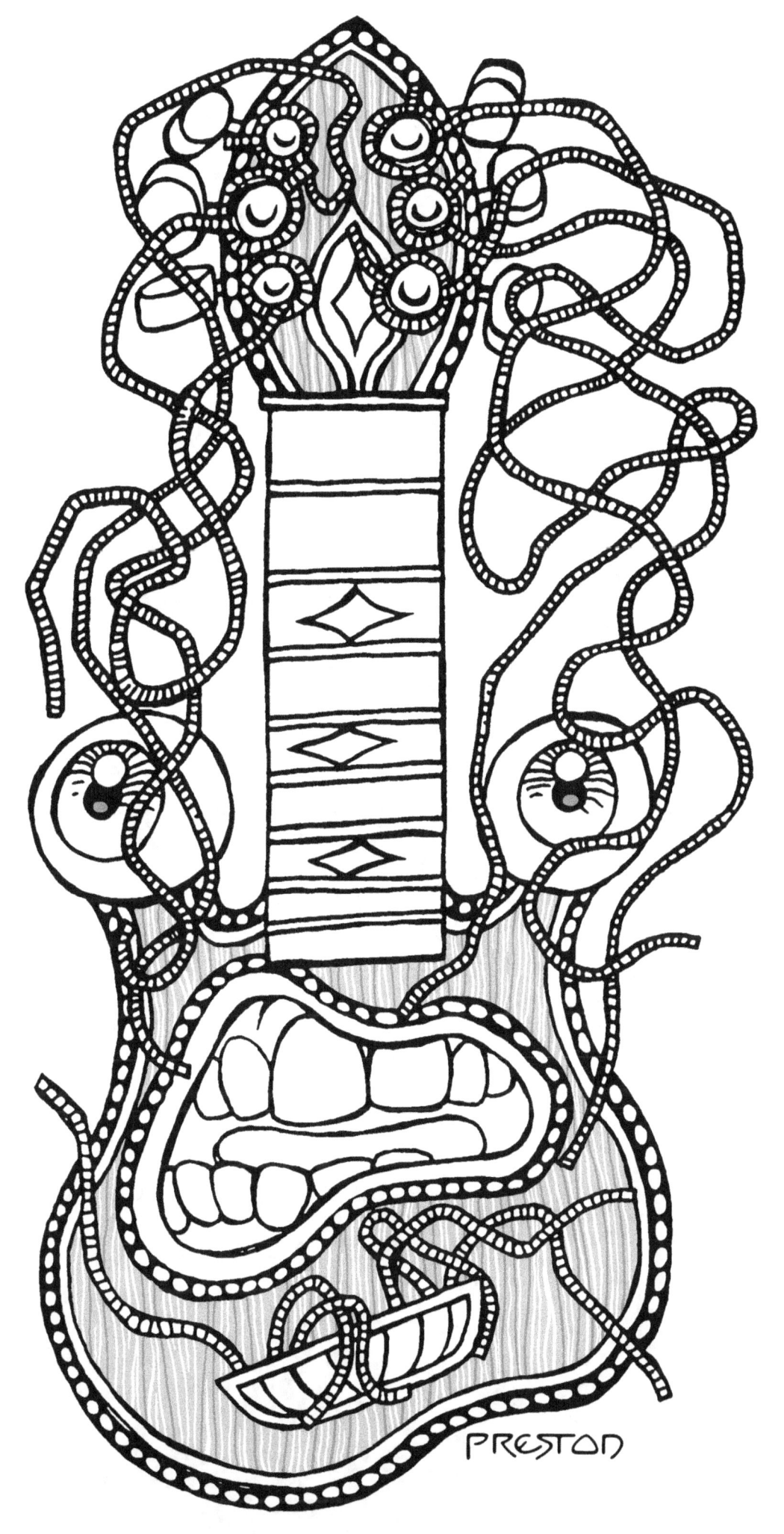

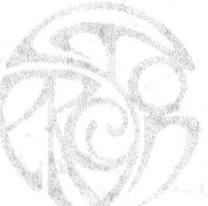

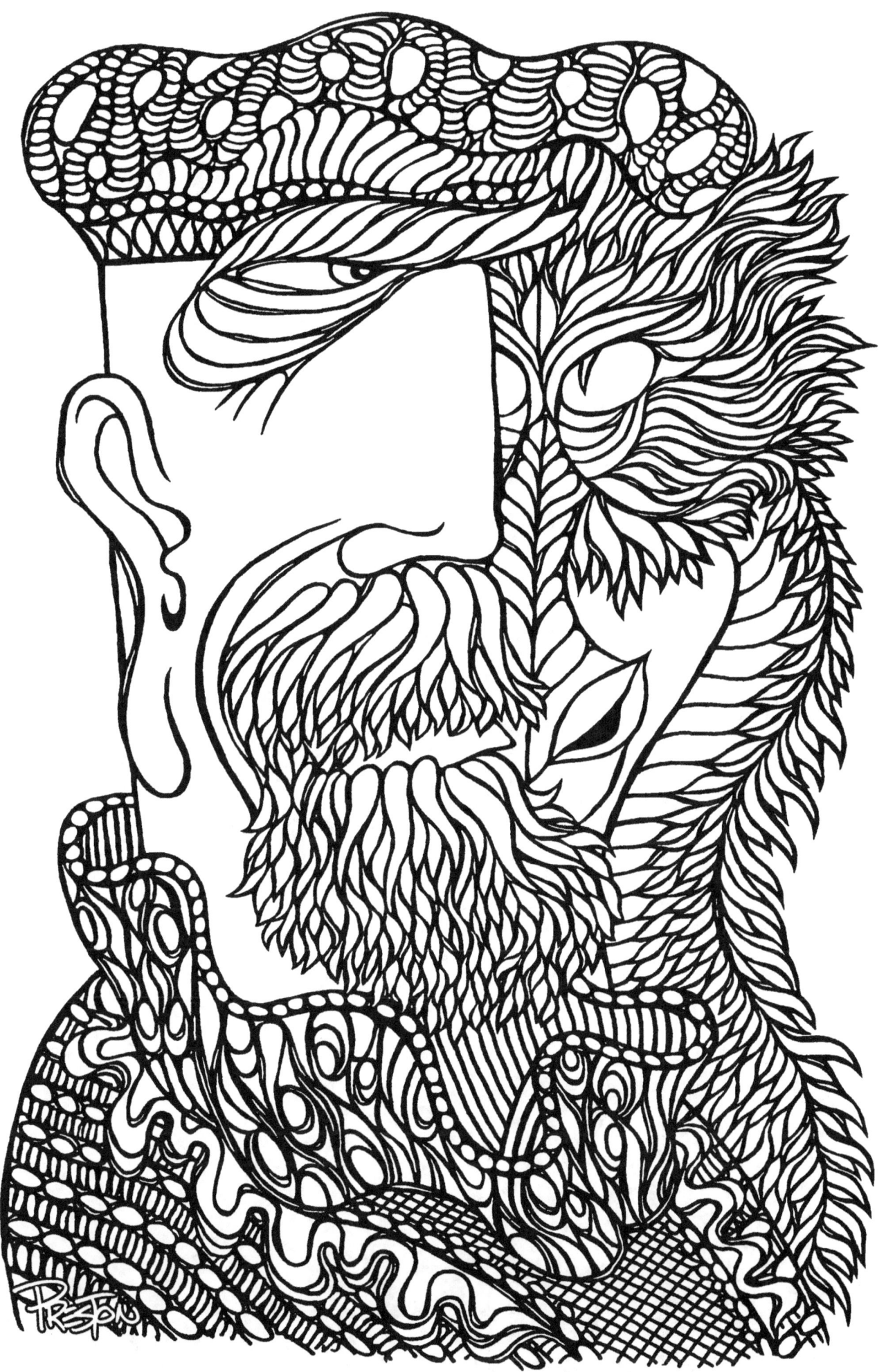

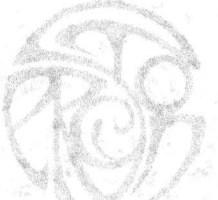

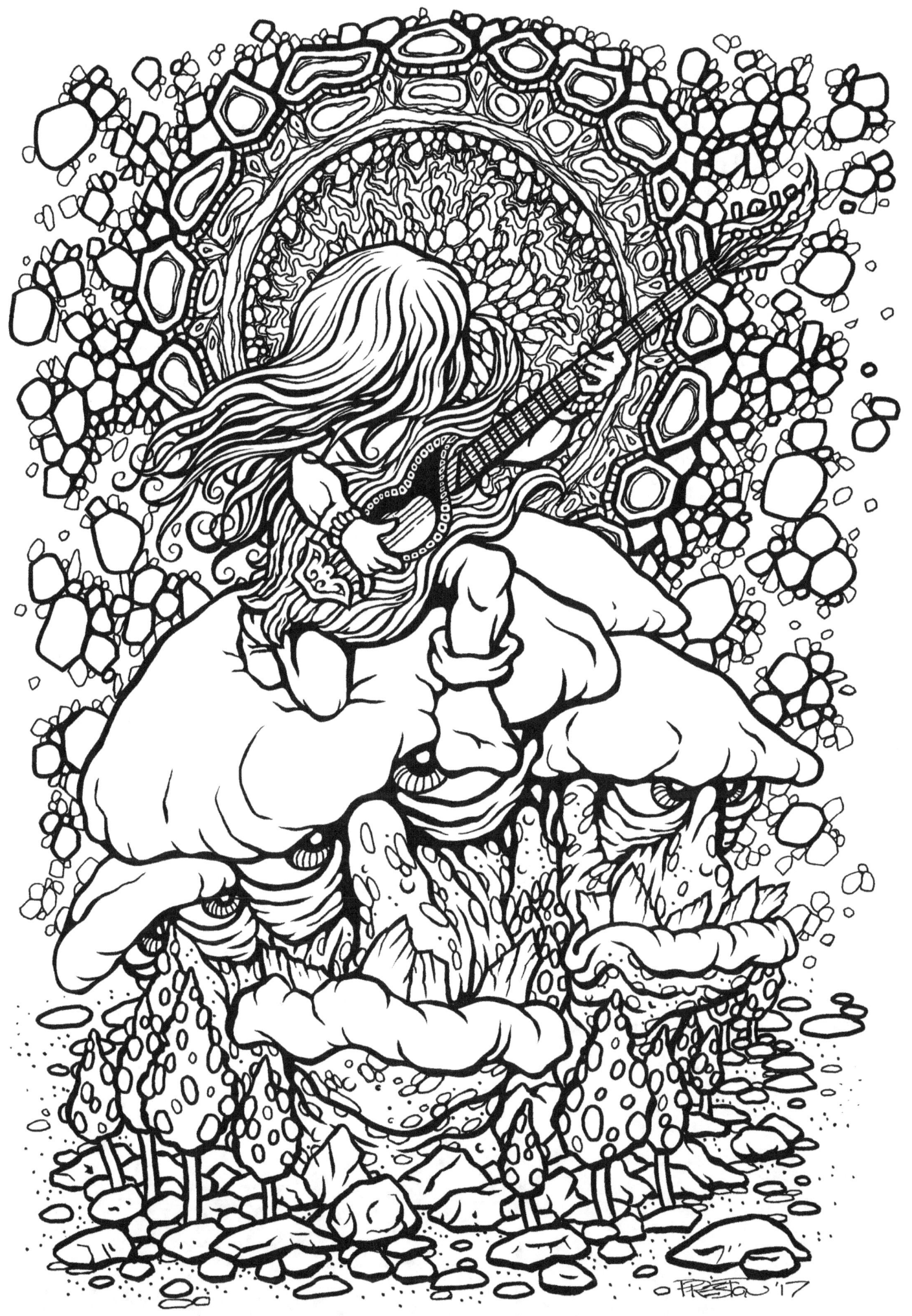

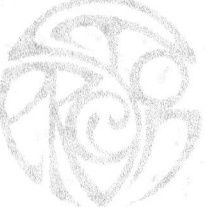

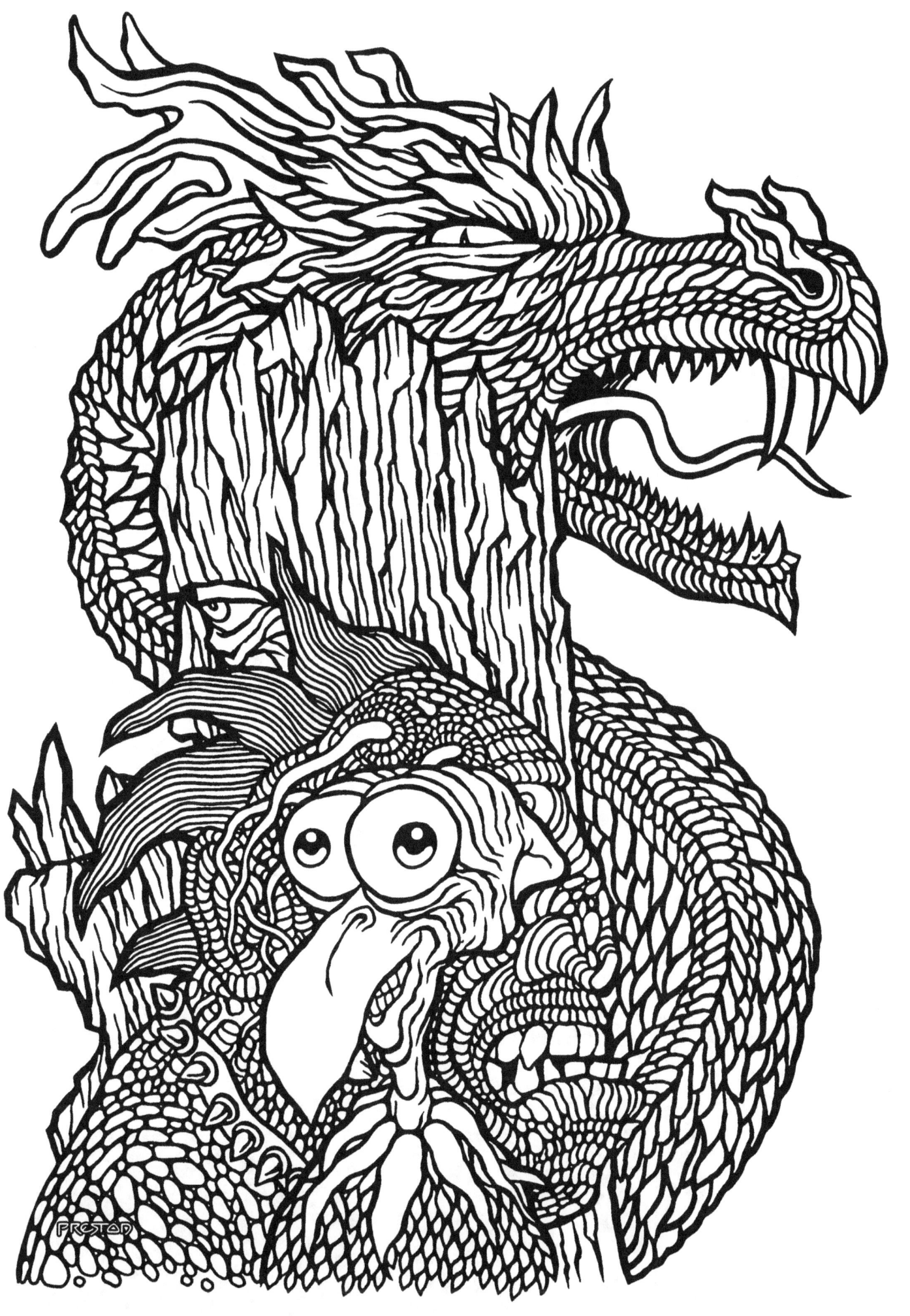

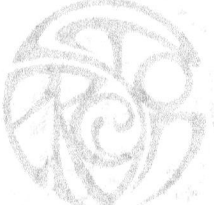

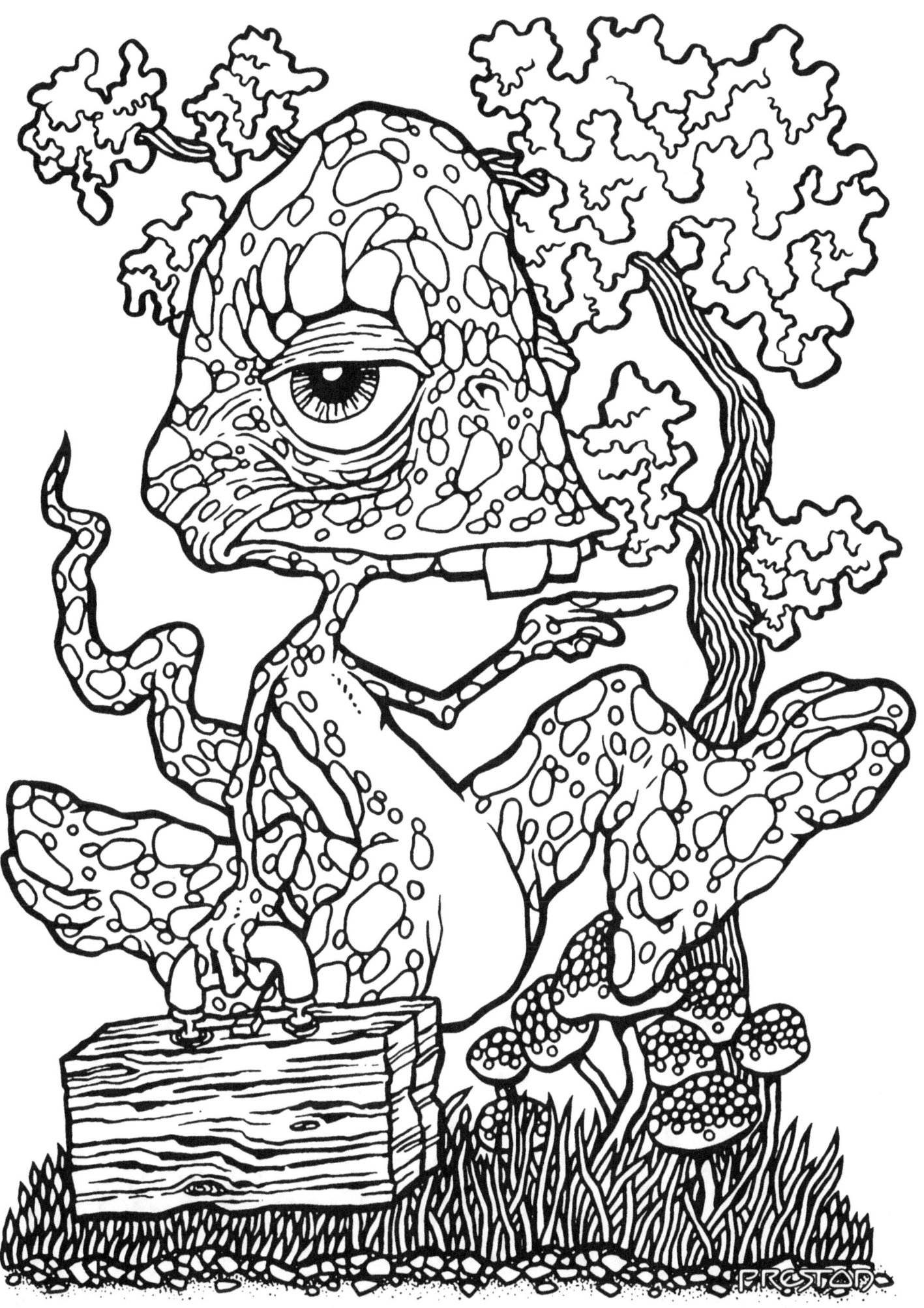

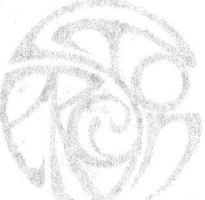

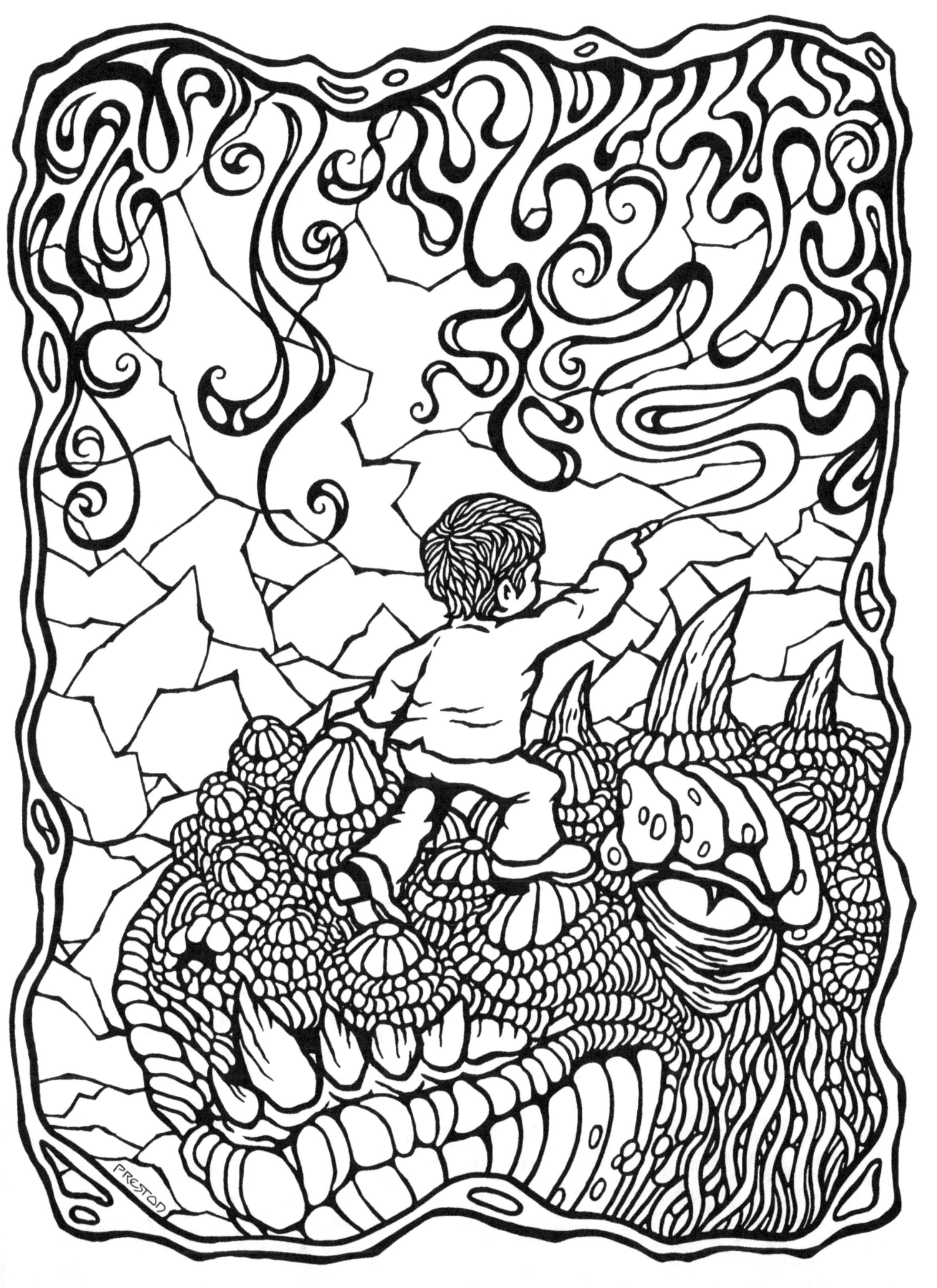

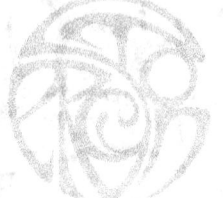

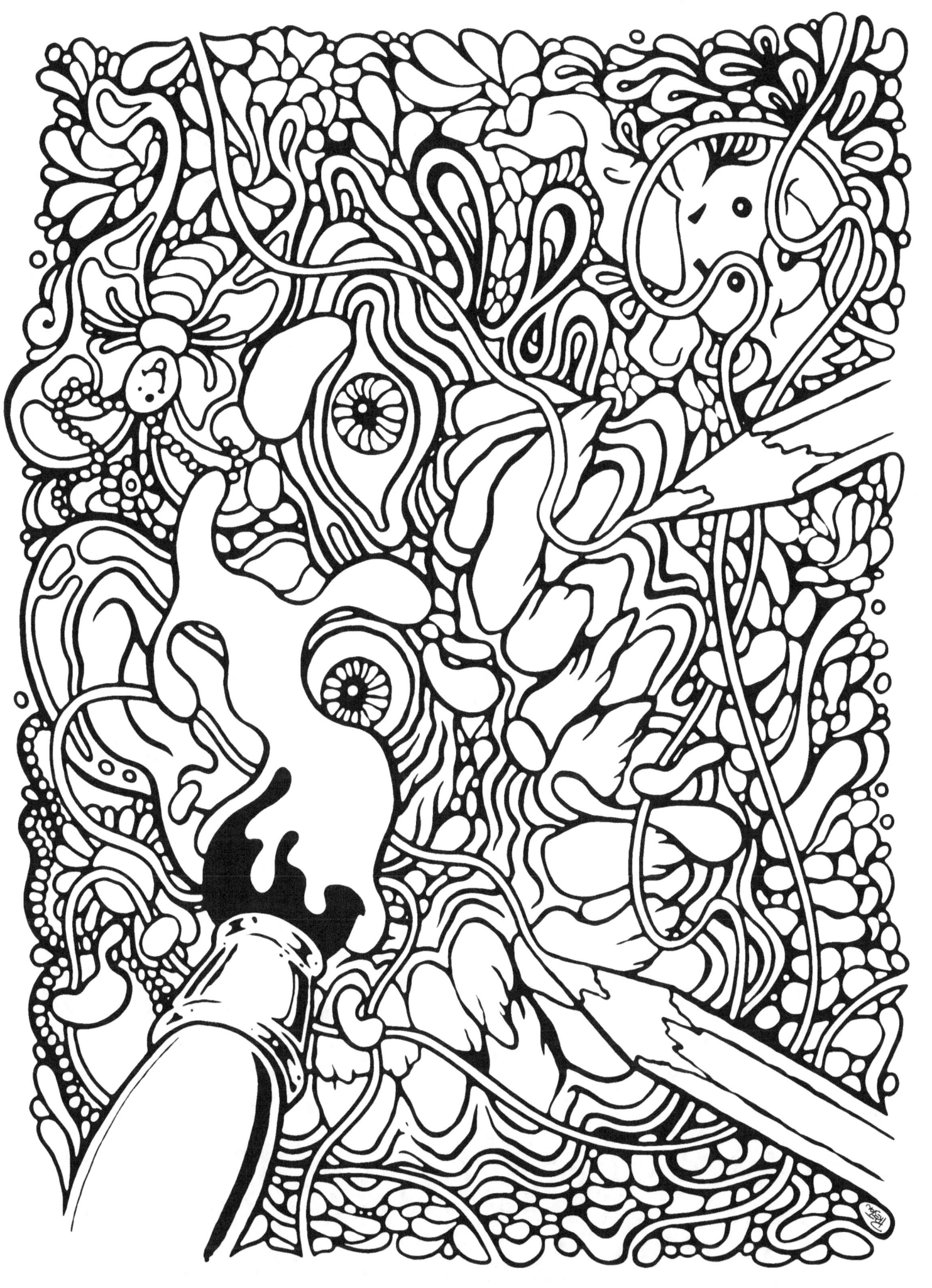

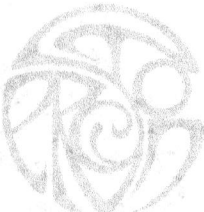

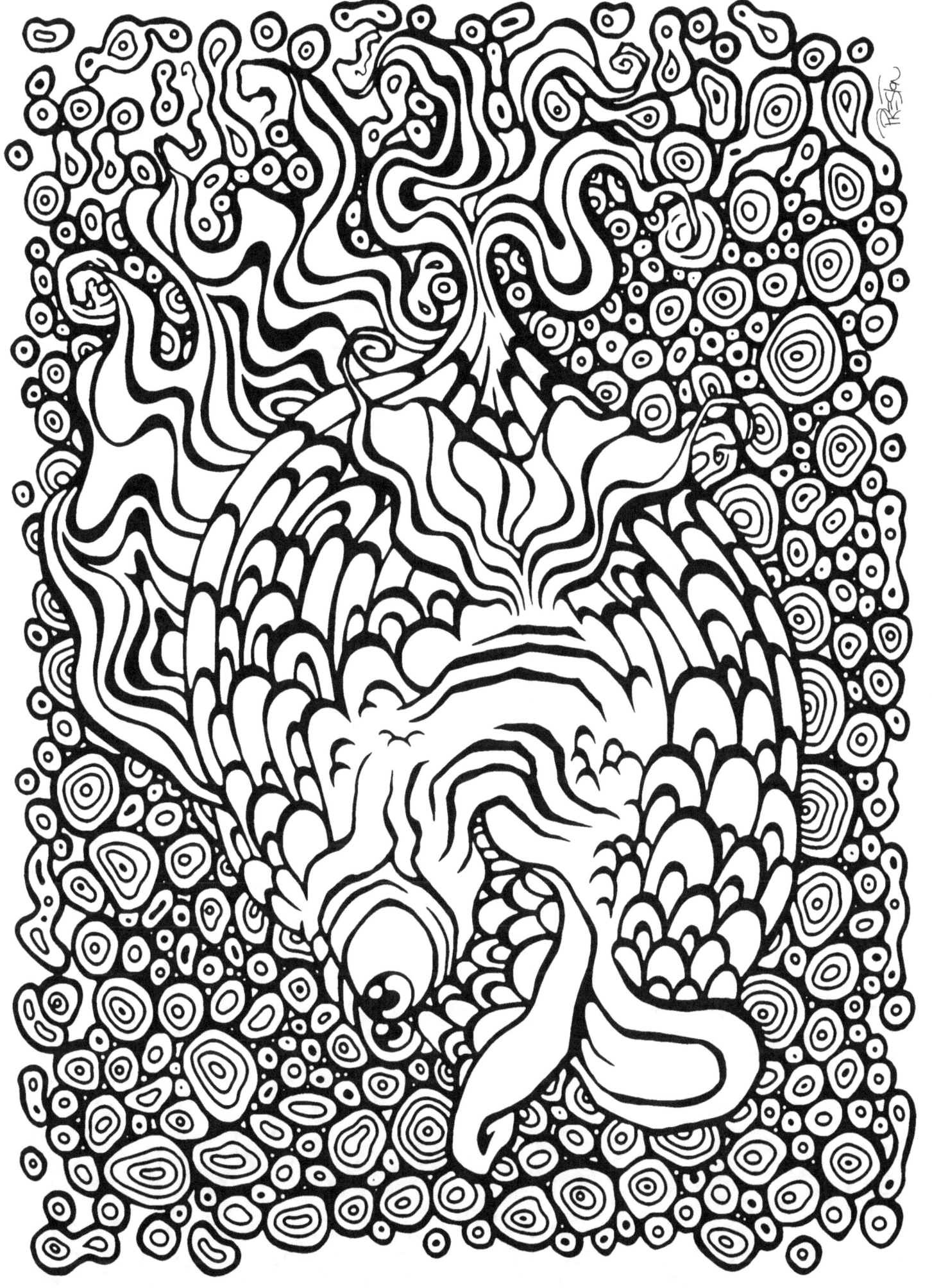

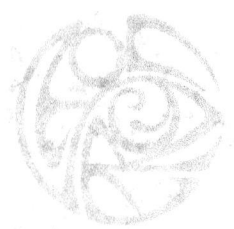

www.ingramcontent.com/pod-product-compliance
Lightning Source LLC
Chambersburg PA
CBHW060011210526
45170CB00017B/2308